HUMAN RESOURCES CHANGES THE WORLD

HOW AND WHY HR AND
HR DIRECTORS SHOULD
STEP-UP AS LEA
IN THE 21ST CEN

GLENN G JONES
FCIPD

Human Resources Changes the World

First published in 2018 by

Panoma Press Ltd
48 St Vincent Drive, St Albans, Herts, AL1 5SJ, UK
info@panomapress.com
www.panomapress.com

Book layout by Neil Coe.

Printed on acid-free paper from managed forests.

ISBN 978-1-784521-41-7

The right of Glenn G Jones to be identified as the author of this work has been asserted in accordance with sections 77 and 78 of the Copyright, Designs and Patents Act 1988.

A CIP catalogue record for this book is available from the British Library.

This book is available online and in bookstores.

Dedication

To my wife Debra,
my daughters Cadence and Megan
and my son Evan.
Thank you for believing in me.

Contents

Introduction

How this book started

Human Resources Changes The World – How and Why HR and HR Directors Should Step-Up as Leaders in the 21st Century

For many years as we progressed into the 21st century, it amazed me as to why CEOs and Boards around the world seemed to make the same mistakes time and time again. As a result, I became interested in understanding why, if people are so crucial to the culture, existence, longevity and prosperity of companies, all too often they were treated like expendable pawns on a chessboard. Also, I was curious, as a Human Resources professional, about what part HR and HR Directors (HRDs) were playing in this game as I truly believe that "HR can change the world".

So, in 2014, I took it upon myself to approach the University of Derby in order to study for a PhD in what I considered would be a game-changer, not only for HR, but for companies, future CEOs, Boards and shareholders.

I was asked to write 10,000 words, just to get the idea up to a good submission standard; unfortunately, as a freelance consultant with very little time at that point in my life, I put the PhD on hold. However, the problem as I saw it kept nagging at me, and as time went on, I was really surprised that no one was really tackling this issue.

Then one day in 2017 in the lounge at Amsterdam airport, I was talking to Stephen Brown of Accenture and he said to me, "Why don't you write a book about it instead?" So, I did. "Why?" you may ask. To enable me to do several things – and before you ask, no, money wasn't one of them.

I have written this book to address the following:

1. To enable Human Resources to evolve to a place that would absolutely make a difference at the highest level.

2. To tackle the imbalance in today's boardrooms in order to tangibly make a difference to companies' employees and their families.

3. To evoke and stimulate the right conversations or debates relating to everyone's role and not solely those in HR.

4. To provide me with a springboard to take this work forward so that I could complete the PhD that I had put on hold.

There you go; that's where the idea for this book came from and how it came to life.

I would like to thank everyone who contributed to this book from around the globe, especially those people whom I was able to interview, including Richard Hill, Patrick Toms, Rebecca Wassell, Marleen van Wouwe, Sarah Hughes, Ben Worthington, Andrew Martin and Darren Lees who shared their thoughts and reflections with me throughout the book. In addition, I would like to thank the quoted authors and other contributors for their support. I hope you enjoy reading it and if nothing else, it's just my view on the world based on empirical data that I was able to assimilate through interviews, observations, and a genuine passion to truly make a difference.

CHAPTER 1

HR DIRECTORS, BOARDS AND CEO BLIND SPOTS

Everyone has a blind spot, no matter if you are a well-paid Chief Executive Officer (CEO) or a cleaner. The key is knowing where yours is and how to address it.

This book aims to really look at Human Resources and Human Resource Directors (HRDs) to understand why moving from HRD to CEO level has always been an almost impossible thing to achieve. We are going to look at the blind spots of those at all levels, from schools all the way up to CEO level, to highlight what needs to happen in the future to ensure that HR does indeed change the world. In addition, we will take a look at how other functions grow their leaders.

For the purpose of this book, included in the abbreviation of HRD is the title of Chief HR Officer (CHRO) and the trendy title of Global People Director (GPD). We will also be looking at Boards and Operating Executives under the catch-all term of Boards or Board.

There are seven questions which this book will address, and rather than neatly laying them out in a table in Chapter 1, I am purposely embedding them in this first chapter to lure you in. Don't worry, they are not difficult to find; in fact, here are the first five:

1. Why is it almost impossible to move from an HRD to CEO level and what research – or more importantly, lack of research – has driven me to write this book?

2. What can HRDs do to bring back parity in the boardroom?

3.   Why don't HRDs make the transition to CEO whilst other Board Members do?

4.   How can HRDs be equipped with the behaviours, competencies and skills required to really add value in the boardroom and to step-up?

5.   Ultimately, we will consider what needs to happen more broadly than HR in order to make the jump to becoming a CEO ahead of one's peers.

Upfront apologies: I am conscious when writing this book that I may alienate myself against the very people I want to help, so please stay with me and I hope to make it up to you. If you aspire to reach the top job – or maybe you don't – this book may drive you to a different career path that you had never considered. If nothing else, it may cause you to consider the world around you and to question why nothing has been done about this before.

Much academic research has been carried out on these issues, and I am pleased to have been able to bring a lot of it together in order to support my beliefs; although I cannot reproduce it word for word, links are set out in the bibliography for more information.

My final apology is that this first chapter is fairly intense with lots of things thrown in; this is obviously deliberate as I seek to set out the context of the issues as I see them.

What my research brought to the surface

HR Magazine (**1**) (author David Woods; November 2011) www.hrmagazine.co.uk/article-details/is-a-move-from-hr-director-to-chief-executive-a-bridge-too-far

The first few paragraphs of this really interesting article called simply, "Is a move from **HR** Director to Chief Executive a bridge too far?" began as follows:

"Can you imagine what it would be like if your HR director ran your business? Would it be a strategic forward-thinking utopia – or a backwater that focussed on tissues, teabags and time and attendance?"

As you read the article, David Woods re-affirms the whole reason why I felt this book was so important. He talks about how it doesn't bode well for **HR** Directors attaining that top position and he mentions that comments regarding **HR** "not being strategic enough" or "doesn't have the business acumen" might have been right or excusable fifteen years ago, but not so today. I especially liked his reference to the Financial Times Stock Exchange (FTSE) 100 and how **HR** has played a part. But that comes out in later research which I will touch upon.

In the same article, the author comments on research published by recruitment company Robert Half International, showing that financial skills are "key" to becoming a CEO. In fact, its survey of the FTSE 100 found that 49% of CEOs had a financial background! Also, during my research, it became clear that CEOs and Boards of today are not fully utilising the experience of HRDs, especially those that had a growth strategy.

So, here's another aim of this book:

6.   To understand why CEOs and Boards don't see HRDs in the CEO succession plan.

At least, they didn't back in 2011 in the United Kingdom when this survey was carried out! I will let you make up your own mind at the end of this book as to whether anything has changed since.

Actually, Janet Candido's (**2**) article entitled "Why HR expertise is a critical addition to your Board" in *The Globe and Mail*, published 19th May 2017, stated the following:

"While the Directors are all very competent professionals, well-versed in their areas of speciality, they had never thought to question issues of human capital. They focused on the business side of things, believing that the CEO was on top of the people issues. There was no HR expertise on this Board, a mistake that led to some costly missteps. Had an independent HR leader been involved, he/she would have seen the signs; increased turnover, difficulty hiring top talent."

"Turnover" in the above context refers to the number of people leaving and joining a company which in itself, massively impacts on the "bottom line".

Janet Candido's article is a great example of what is going wrong right now in business and, if you recall from the Introduction, is one of the reasons for writing this book. Boards are simply missing the fact that having the right people at the top really does make a difference. How? I hear you asking. Well it's not just in a financial sense and the bottom line, it's also reputational, together with the impact on employee engagement, culture and diversity.

Ironically, one thing that was really evident to me during the recession years following 2008, and even now in the late 2010s and moving forward into the 2020s, is how so many CEOs and Boards choose to ignore the advice and guidance of their HRDs. It's been almost 20 years since the immortal words (yes sadly I am going to say it) were coined regarding "The war for talent" (**3**) *(Steven Hankin of McKinsey and Co; 1997)* but still we see companies and organisations all around the world forgetting the importance of their greatest **assets** – their employees/people/staff – when making substantial strategic changes.

That said, Lucy Adams, (former **BBC HR Director**) in her 2017 book *HR Disrupted* (**4**) wrote something on page 39 which was very apt about how we describe employees as assets:

"Something I've noticed over the years is employers lack the right terminology to describe their employees; if they're not referring to them as family (which, as we've seen isn't appropriate), they're talking about them as assets. What an awful term."

Lucy is absolutely right and points to one of the main problems of the way companies are treating their people. The very terminology used is, I believe, offensive, and as Lucy says, they are seen "as a homogenous lump".

By the way, if you weren't sure of the meaning of homogenous (**5**):

Homogeneous ˌhɒmə(ʊ)ˈdʒiːnɪəs, ˌhəʊmə(ʊ)ˈdʒiːnɪəs/

of the same kind; alike. "If all jobs and workers were homogeneous".

She then goes on to consider and provide a refreshing look at employees as consumers and what would happen potentially to HR if this view were taken:

"HR leaders would develop a deep level of insight into their people.

"This would encourage them to move away from a one-size-fits-all approach to employees.

"They would therefore design their procedures and processes around the users instead of themselves."

We may touch on this concept of a 'homogenous lump' more in the following chapters, so look out for this. However, this isn't solely an item for HR to resolve; today there's a huge blind spot in many companies and Boards to even acknowledge that their greatest competitive advantage is their people.

This then links us to aim number 7:

7. Why does the above attitude still manifest itself as a consistent theme and why haven't Boards and CEOs realised its impact on those companies, their workforce and more importantly, their bottom line as a result of this? Why have Boards and CEOs not embraced "HRness"?

Yes, I know I've created a new word, but here is my definition of "HRness":

"Our people who work for us are really important, and instead of paying lip service and downgrading HR, we should be enhancing our people capabilities and the focus shouldn't be solely on the financials or the technology. Once again, we have forgotten the 'human' part of HR."

From early on in my career, I noticed that the most effective HRDs had something different about them. I recall attending a dinner hosted by the Chartered Institute of Payroll Professionals back in 2003 (the guest speaker was the retiring HRD from British Telecom) and I remember he said something that was very profound to me; he was asked what made him so different from other HR Directors and he said something which stayed with me until today. Quite simply it was the fact that he was different from his other HR professionals who were less commercial. Furthermore, he went on to say that his other HR Director peers were less business focused and even though they said they partnered with the business that they worked for, they really didn't from the point of truly driving the business forward which manifested itself in a lack of credibility.

Fourteen years on, I was consulting with Imperial Tobacco where Richard Hill (a great guy and a role model), the then new Group Transformation and HR Director, exhibited the same noticeable unique selling points. Of course, I'm not going to share it with you now, but it will come out later in this book as I was fortunate enough to have had the chance to interview Richard to gain better insight into what made him so very different (you might want to check out Richard's career at some stage as it's very interesting) from other HR Directors that I have known.

So, let's come back and examine the definition of 'blind spot'. The *Oxford English Dictionary* (**6**) states:

'an area in which a person lacks understanding or impartiality.'

Ironically, to date, I could not find any academic material on HRDs' blind spots, nor the reasons why some HRDs were seen as ineffective in the boardroom during things like restructures, but I have been able to find a few online articles that touched on this. Also, nothing at all on HRDs becoming CEOs appeared in academic research, but again, a few online articles suggested that this does happen.

Now, I know that I am making a big statement here and I also know that there are some great HRDs out there who really are masters in the boardroom, although sadly they are a rarity in my opinion. That said, they are out there. For example, in 2014, Mary Barra, previously Global HR VP, became CEO of General Motors. (Mary came into HR via other areas of GM and went to university to study Electrical Engineering). Ann Mulcahey served as CHRO at Xerox; John Hofmeister, US HRD, went on to become President of Shell Oil; Martyn Phillips became CEO of B&Q following his role as Operations and HR Director. So what enabled these people to make the jump?

Let's take a moment to look at 'understanding' or 'impartiality'. What is it that an HRD lacks from an understanding or an impartiality perspective? What makes them so different from their other colleagues on the Board that they are so easily dismissed, when the reality is that they should be the trusted adviser to the CEO and the gatekeeper to keeping the rest of the Board in check? Is it as Marshall Goldsmith said in his book *Triggers* (**7**) something to do with the environment (see p31) or is it as he goes on to say:

"At many companies, HR is solely an administrative responsibility – HR people are keepers of the employee handbook – with little influence over the company's direction and strategy" (p84).

This wasn't the only reference to HR being seen purely as an administrative tool either; Edward E Lawler III and John W Boudreau (**8**) in their 2015 book *Achieving Excellence in Human Resources Management – An Assessment of Human Resources Functions* quoted:

"All too often, the human resources function is largely an administrative function headed by individuals whose roles are focused on cost control and administrative activities" (p4).

To reinforce this, the following table from Lawler and Boudreau's updated 2015 version clearly demonstrates the percentage of time spent on various HR roles by country/ geography:

HR Role	US	Canada	Australia	Europe	UK	India	China
Maintaining records	15.2	17.9	12.7	22.3	15.9	19.1	23.7
Auditing/ controlling	13.0	9.9	14.0	13.5	11.0	14.4	16.6
HR service provider	25.7	36.4	28.2	24.6	28.1	26.0	28.1
Development of HR systems and practices	19.0	15.8	17.3	16.5	16.3	20.2	18.0
Strategic business partner	27.1	19.9	27.9	23.1	28.7	20.2	13.7

It is interesting that there is a direct correlation between those countries/geographies that spend less on the strategic business partnering role and instead choose to spend more time on maintaining records and auditing/ controlling the business.

Goldsmith (**7**) (p94) also writes about Alicia, an HRD who was invited to the Board by, what I would consider, a wise CEO because he knew that with so many employees in his company, his Head of Human Resources would make or break it. We will come back to Marshall Goldsmith's story about Alicia later in the book to see what she did to make a difference and why she became successful (see Chapter 6.)

At the time of compiling the research for this book, the Chartered Institute of Personnel and Development (CIPD) in their *People Management* magazine (**9**) (March 2017, p25) led with their primary article which, ironically, was entitled "How to Be Top Dog – What great HR leaders do and how to follow in their footsteps"! The article called out things like:

1. Education – 70% of good HR leaders had a degree or degree-level qualifications in Business or Human Resources.

2. Highly developed Emotional Intelligence (EQ) – all skilled HR professionals have in common a highly developed EQ and a natural ability to sense how the people they work with are feeling, and the right times to deploy initiatives.

3. Strength of Integrity – as Dr Stephen Moir (Chief People Office, NHS England) says – "A lot of what good HRDs do doesn't get seen."

4. Change Management and Organisational Design – between 20 to 25% specialise in this area.

So, in summing up the article, my belief is that we weren't setting a new bar but doing more of the same. Also, the article didn't address how HRDs should evolve, sadly, nor did it address the leap to becoming the next CEO. Eight years prior to the writing of the article, again referring to Lawler and Boudreau's 2009 (**11**) book (p4), they called out the following:

"To be strategic partners, HR executives need an expert understanding of business strategy, organisational design, and change management, and they need to know how integrated human resources practices and strategies can support organisation designs and strategies. This role requires extending HR's focus beyond delivery of HR services and practices to focus on quality of decisions about organisational design and human capital (Boudreau and Ramstad 2007)."

Lawler and Boudreau go on to say in their book that HR can bring a different dimension and view to the board, specifically because of HR's insight into the companies' people. But again, this is missed or not understood by boards and once again, nothing changes.

Ask yourself this question: how many of your company's strategies have failed because of the fact that HR was not involved, or the CEO didn't have an HR background? Then ask yourself the question why?

Having read the last two paragraphs, I leave it up to you to judge how good the CIPD article was and where you see the blind spots.

Let's move this on a little and consider some of Lawler and Boudreau's other research (**8**) (p16):

"Why do some firms continue to place executives in charge of human resources functions who are not 'traditional' human resources

executives? There are three likely reasons. First, senior executives without any HR background are being put in charge of HR in order to develop them because they are a candidate for the CEO job. Second, they are being put in charge of HR in order to make it run more like a business and be more of a business partner. Third, failed line managers are being put into HR because it is a 'safe' pre-retirement job."

Some interesting comments indeed from the guys, and certainly my ears pricked up when I saw the reference to a potential CEO candidate! However, this was short-lived when I re-read the words "without any HR background" but as the above stated, this was based on speculation and not hard facts. It does raise the question though, of how HR and HRD roles in particular are viewed by companies, and again, I leave this up to you to answer and draw your own conclusions. That said, it would be remiss of me if I didn't give my own view and I think this is a blind spot that can be dealt with quickly if given the right energy and direction from the top.

Earlier in the chapter, I touched on the interview that I had with Richard Hill which presented me with another blind spot observation that I hadn't considered before. When I asked Richard why HRDs don't make the jump to CEO, he stated that "it would be unlikely for a Board to go for someone who had not been a CEO before, a salesman or a proven Chief Financial Officer (CFO)".

So, this offered up another potential blind spot if Richard was indeed correct. He went on to say:

"Having a commercial (financial) background is essential as any executive team is looking to deliver value and return for their shareholders. Business 'nous' is massively important. If you don't get this, then you will not be credible."

Therefore, unless an HRD has been a CFO or has been clearly seen to have delivered value before, does this mean that they will never be able to make the jump? Or does it mean that to enable someone from an HR background to make the move, they have to cross-train or skill-up in the finance arena? Let's look at this later in the book to see where else HRDs may have gaps in their kit bags of skills, experience and knowledge or whether it is about not being focused on today, to give you the roadmap to becoming a CEO of the future.

Another blind spot that Richard brought up was that the HRD must be a business leader and be curious around people and to be able to think through how leaders impact on the humans in their company. A sensitivity to the organisation that they are part of and a curiosity around people and how they behave. This was an interesting statement by Richard as one would assume the Director of Human Resources should be first and foremost someone who understands and is curious about people. So, reflecting back to the CIPD article earlier, my view was that this wasn't touched on apart from, I guess, if they say they are being "empathic" but I don't believe they meant the same.

Earlier on, I touched on Martyn Phillips' appointment to CEO from HRD at B&Q and in the article in *HR Magazine,* (**10**) he stated the following which, for me, is another blind spot of boards and existing CEOs:

"At B&Q, our people are our biggest asset – that is what makes us so successful. As HR Director, I was responsible for employing a strong and diverse workforce, and so I gained strong people and interpersonal skills, as well as being the best coach I can be to employees. A good sense of all aspects of the company's operation is also a vital quality to have if making the move to CEO – they are valuable skills which I have transferred to my new role as CEO of B&Q."

Martyn went on to say in his comments that the skills required for CEOs are not that much different to those for HRDs. However, in Chapter 5 we will see if that is right or not (please don't jump forward.) One thing where I am aligned with Martyn is the belief that both an HRD and a great CEO must "be able to shape an organisation and achieve profitability through leveraging the workforce."

It's funny how things start to come into line when you start researching a book like this! There was a very good article that made it onto LinkedIn regarding Uber's CEO, Travis Kalanick, who basically had to resign over allegations of staff abuse and alleged law-breaking (not my comments by the way). The article by Arthur Goldstuck **(12)** (https://www.businesslive.co.za/bt/opinion/2017-06-24-arthur-goldstuck-uber-chaos-brings-humanity-to-depersonalised-tech/) stated the following:

"Technology firms and innovators are waking up to the realisation that technology advances should not be made at the expense of people and values."

In the same article Arthur wrote:

"Any CEO that doesn't put people first is leading a failed cause," said SAP CEO Bill McDermott in a closing keynote address.

"In the next five years, you'll see more chief human resources officers become CEOs than in the prior 50 years, because today you have to have people skills to succeed in business.

"If you don't have people in your veins, in your DNA, you can't succeed."

While studying for my Executive 7 Institute of Learning Managing qualification, I remember attending a training course re conscious vs subconscious behaviour. During the course, the lecturer asked had we ever settled on buying a certain make of car and then, all of a sudden, that car appears everywhere? In the same vein, it seemed to ring true as I started to pull this book together: more and more sources/people were starting to wake up to HRDs becoming CEOs. I guess we will see how the book progresses.

Another point that started to manifest itself during my research was cemented when I interviewed Patrick Toms (then Head of Organisational Effectiveness, Global Reward and Capability at Imperial). Patrick commented that HR has a broader challenge with a level of pessimism and a victim mentality as to why there is no HR seat at the Board table. Patrick went on to say that he thought that "HR is doomed and in years to come, HR administration will be outsourced and the strategic element embedded in other functional units."

Is he right? (Ironically, you will see more comments like this further in the book so look out for them). Only time will tell I guess. My view, while we are dealing with human beings, is that we will always need a function that strategically and operationally drives this forward; it may be called something else of course until machines and Artificial Intelligence take over, which is always a possibility.

Patrick, ironically, was a great example of someone without any formal HR background but with excellent business credentials formed during his roles outside of HR. At the time of writing this book, he was being promoted into an HRD role in Germany with Imperial. You can probably see a bit of a pattern emerging in the book already, but let's not jump to any conclusions at this stage.

We continued our conversation and another blind spot that Patrick surfaced was around the leadership development of HR leaders. HR as a function spends a great deal of its time helping other functions in development areas but it appears less driven in seeking leadership qualities for itself. For example, of the HR Executive at Imperial (strategic HR leadership team) at the time, only one person out of the six-strong team had had formal leadership development, and that was before they made it onto the HR Executive (this term is often shorted to HR Exec or HR Leadership Team (HRLT).

So, was Lucy Adams right when she said in her book *HR Disrupted* (p7) (**4**) that "HR is no longer fit for purpose?" Well it seems that unless something radical happens, she may be right… or is she?

Summary and recap

During the course of this first chapter, we have highlighted the main aims of this book:

1. To discuss why HRDs, boards and CEOs don't see the current blind spots.

2. What HRDs can do to bring back parity in the boardroom.

3. To consider why it is that HRDs never make the transition to CEO whilst other Board Members do.

4. To provide HRDs the behaviours, competencies and skills required to really add value in the boardroom.

5. Ultimately to consider what needs to happen in order to make the jump to becoming a CEO ahead of their peers.

6. To understand why CEOs and Boards don't see HRDs in the CEO succession plan.

7. To ask why is it a consistent theme that companies do not realise their greatest asset is their people, and why haven't Boards realised the impact on their companies, their workforce and more importantly their bottom line as a result of this?

We have drawn on academic research, online articles and specific interviews to highlight what is out there – which isn't a great deal. For me personally there are a few specific items to note:

- There is a view that a purist HR administrator will never be able to make it to CEO unless they… (see later in the book.)

- Human Resources personnel and departments are not, on the whole, taken seriously in the boardroom.

- While an HRD can be a confidante to a CEO, there is a perception that purist HRDs don't have the relevant business skills.

- Human Resources hasn't moved forward (as per Lawler and Boudreau's research) and still shows a huge amount of time being spent on the lower end of the role rather than targeting the high-end value-add to the business in supporting strategic events, moves etc.

- There must be some great examples of purist HRDs who have made the jump to CEO, but their numbers are much fewer than CEOs who have come from other functions like accounting, sales, engineering or manufacturing etc. Sadly though, at the time of writing this book, I was unable to source any more examples than those you will read in these pages.

- Human Resources institutions like the CIPD haven't acknowledged or addressed why HRDs don't move to become CEOs; instead they regurgitate more of the same. They opt for the still fluffy alternatives which, in my opinion, keep HR back in the dark ages.

CHAPTER 2

TRADITIONAL ROUTE TO BECOMING AN HRD

For many years since the inception of HR as a function and as a distinct role, the vast majority of people who have an HR role somewhere in their work history have either gone to university to do something like a master's in Human Resources Management (I'm going to take a leap here and say that this is probably the minority) or else they have "fallen" into HR, ie they gained an admin role and worked their way up (again, I believe that this is the route most people have travelled.) One thing is for sure: I don't think four- or five-year-old children say, "I know I am going to be the best or world-class Human Resources Director which will then enable me to become a CEO in any industry."

I can say this from personal experience; when I go into schools today, most children and teenagers don't even know what HR is. If they do, it is probably because their parents have worked in HR, or they have had a run-in with HR and therefore their understanding is based on that; if that's the case, then who knows what view they have of HR!

If you look at the best advertisement for HR in the world, it's probably the CIPD (formed in 1913) based primarily in the UK (https://www.cipd.co.uk/.) I'm not wishing to criticise here but even that wasn't granted its Royal Charter until July 2000 so this kind of gives you a clue to how it compares with the Association of Certified Chartered Accountants (**ACCA**) (**13**) which was formed in 1904 but gained its Royal Charter in 1974! No wonder then, HR is lagging thirty years behind its comparator in the accountancy world. Enough said from the Chartered Fellow of the CIPD before I get myself into trouble!

So now we are starting to get a picture of the problem; it all starts with how children look at their future and dream of getting to the top. I am pretty sure that HR is not high on their priority list, so how can we change this? My answer would be to promote HR within schools, to explain to teenagers why it's absolutely needed in business and to give them another option instead of Accountancy and Information Technology. If you are reading this as an HR professional, I leave it to you to take up this challenge. I am trying to do my part by joining the Board of Governors at my daughter's school, a great way of giving back but also ironically, another way of influencing.

It's probably a subject for another book but I was surprised to see the lack of HR representation on my daughter's school's Board of Governors, hence why I joined and quickly took up the role of Chair.

Back to the topic at hand. So, let's paint a picture of what happens in these different scenarios:

Person A – The "fall" into HR and the path to HRD

This, for me, is the most likely scenario that has presented itself in the past. Our 'Person A' leaves school or further education after studying something completely unrelated but lands their first job as an HR administrator or some other HR role. They gain their local experience based on how good or bad their line manager is, and stay with the company for a few years. They move into an HR Manager role based on their current experience, then lo and behold, an opportunity arises where the HRD role becomes vacant and, guess what? They get that too. On the other hand, they move up a level in another company or organisation, based on their previous years' experience, rather than following any dedicated HR career plan.

How do I know this? Apart from what I have seen myself over the years, I decided to survey my theory via my network of over 3000 people on LinkedIn (www.linkedin. com). A few phone calls later, I had three great volunteers who agreed to be interviewed on three distinct questions:

1. What did you want to do when you grew up and were you aware of the HR function?

2. How did you get into HR?

3. What do you feel needs to change in HR?

Here are the stories which they agreed to share:

Rebecca Wassell (Associate Director of Transformation, Gloucestershire Hospitals, UK)

"My entry into the field of HR was 'accidental'. Having maintained a highly successful career as a clinical scientist and then in general management in the public sector, with my first managerial appointment at the age of 24, I decided to study full-time for an MBA at Aston University Business School.

"For the dissertation, I wanted to work with an organisation outside of the public sector to gain more commercial experience, and I wrote to the Engineering Employers' Federation asking if they would send a request on my behalf to member companies. They agreed and about a dozen responses came back.

"Some weren't suited to a master's dissertation, but one of the opportunities, at (then) LucasVarity Diesel Systems

---

(now part of Delphi Automotive) was too good to be true. I was interviewed, references were taken, and I was then appointed to develop a self-assessment framework taking current business plans and business performance data, using European Foundation for Quality Management (EFQM) Business Excellence as the base structure. This done, I was to assess the seven European sites and report back to the Board. I had four months.

"It was a brilliant experience and I learned so much from the Board Members and staff alike – lessons, attitudes and behaviours that I will carry for the rest of my working life as my benchmark of people management excellence.

"The project completed, dissertation written and submitted, the Board were keen for me to stay but were reticent to create a new corporate role. As one of the Heads of HR resigned to take up a position elsewhere, I was offered the opportunity to step in. The company believed, from what they had seen, that I would be able to manage this – and to continue with the business excellence programme.

"A career in HR was born.

"Six months later, I was asked to consider a move to the largest Business Unit, to head up and transform HR. This was a brave move by the company as I had so little direct HR experience, but they saw in me someone who understood business and who could translate this into people strategy and management.

"I have never looked back. In the past 19 years, I have been able to seamlessly move from sector to sector, industry to industry. I have had the opportunity to engage at a high level with industry and business organisations as a council member, or as chair of steering and strategic committees. A huge debt of gratitude is due to those people at LucasVarity who took such a gamble two decades ago on that rookie practitioner."

Marleen van Wouwe (HR Director Imperial Brands, BeNeLux)

"I cannot recall ever mentioning aspiring to a certain role as a child, mostly knowing what I didn't want to do (teacher, nurse) and looking for something where I could apply logic and work with others.

"Therefore, after leaving school and not really knowing what profession would be the right one for me, I chose to start a general study at university, assuming this would keep a lot of options open.

"Well, it did help me understand what was not my cup of tea. So, the start of my career was leaving university without a diploma, but with debt and still no clue what was the right career choice for me. So, in the early 90s I started in a management support role as an Office Manager. As the company grew, I offered to take on HR tasks and found these were things I liked and turned out to be good at! It gave me the opportunity to move into my first full-time HR role and to study HR in the evenings.

"Over twenty years later, I can still say HR is my place to be. It means I am doing something that fits my capabilities, technical skills, knowledge, influencing and interpersonal skills and passion. All of this has made it possible to move from HR Assistant to HR Officer, working for bigger departments, and finally moving into HR management positions. I've been lucky enough to find my perfect match and have worked with inspiring people along the way!"

Sarah J Hughes, Chartered FCIPD (HR Director SGS Co.)

"What did I want to do when I left school? No idea. The careers advice was shocking and they were pushing 'jobs for girls' – nurses, teachers etc, but the only other option at the time, if you were not going to university, was the Youth Training Scheme (YTS). My parents and grandparents had their own businesses and I knew what hard work was as I had been working for them since I was about 11! I applied for five YTS roles, and following all the interviews, was offered all five, but decided to take the one at Rolls-Royce (RR) and joined as administrator.

"The YTS Scheme was for 12 months and you did four placements; you were also sponsored to do a day-release training programme at college. I did Business Studies – of which HR was part of the curriculum and I also had exposure to the Training & Development Department. After completing my initial training, I moved into the Training Department as Training Administrator supporting Young People Training which covered graduates/apprentices/interns and students doing work experience.

"I finished college and asked RR for further sponsorship which was agreed and I was sponsored to do a Higher National Certificate (HNC) in Business Studies with HR option. I stayed for five years and progressed through the job family, eventually completing my CIPD and recognising I really needed to move into HR.

"Rolls Royce was quite traditional at that time and to progress, you had to work in the 'Functions' that reflected CIPD at the time (Learning & Development, Resourcing and Employee Relations (ER). I moved into a central role combining Resourcing & ER. This included doing all the collective bargaining with the full works and staff committees etc.

"I moved to a managerial role within the operations part of the business and was sponsored to complete an MSc. Since leaving RR in 2008, I have held senior global HR roles."

Three great examples would you not agree? Thanks again to all three in helping me with this book.

In addition to the above, I mentioned that I've read Lucy Adams' book *HR Disrupted* **(4)** Here's what Lucy says in relation to how she learned more about HR in her first management role (p19):

"I listened to the experts on my new team. They told me the way to do remuneration was X and the way to do training was Y; I assumed that they knew best. You could say I swallowed the manual and regurgitated it."

Lucy, by the way, studied History and English Literature at university.

Person B – They went to college or university to study HR and eventually became an HRD

This is the rarer practice where you see someone who actually aspires to go into HR. They go to college or university specifically to learn about HR and begin their career with a junior HR Business Partner Role. Then when an opportunity appears, they are promoted into an HRD role.

Unfortunately (and somewhat ironically) I didn't come across anyone in my survey who fitted this bill, but I am sure that they are out there somewhere, and maybe this is something to be looked at for the next edition.

Person C – The person who goes to college or university for something other than HR, and then is selected via the "milkround" to go on a graduate scheme

A student is attracted by a company to take part in their Graduate Scheme. The "milkround" is the phrase used when a student is picked up by employers coming into universities looking to attract the brightest talent to work for them. This happens especially to those people who are really clever and like working with people. They perform really well and again, eventually get promoted into an HRD role and then probably progress to another role somewhere in the organisation.

If you don't believe me on this one, then the following online article from *The Guardian* (**14**) (Harriet Minter; 30 July 2010) entitled "Routes into HR" starts with the following statement by Georgina Kvassay, HR strategy consultant at the CIPD:

"Popular with both graduates and career changers, HR is about more than just being a 'people person'."

It was by pure chance that I noticed during my time at Imperial that one of their HRDs did actually come through this route. I interviewed Ben Worthington using the same three questions as above. Here's Ben's story and also, his interesting thoughts on the future of HR, plus why he believes HRDs don't get to CEO level.

Ben Worthington (UK&I Imperial HR Director)

"During my school years, my career aspirations were predominantly based around sports, ie to be a rugby player, sports teacher or a physiotherapist, but that wasn't to be!

"So, I went to Bournemouth University where I studied Retail Management which included a small module in HR. It was during my sandwich year that I was fortunate enough to get an HR placement with House of Fraser. This exposed me to some really great people and HR experience predominantly around learning, TUPE (Transfer of Undertakings - Protection of Employment) and some large-scale recruitment.

"Post-university, I gained an HR graduate placement with Airbus (formerly British Aerospace) which was a great and varied introduction to HR, where I was also able to get some CIPD training via an external business school.

"It wasn't until I went to work at Kohler Co. that I really began to develop my business skills; I started to learn more and more about HR in a smaller company by having to be involved in the full remit of HR activity on limited resources. Later, seeing the opposite end of this spectrum by working in Lloyds Bank and TSB, where there were huge levels of resources, has really helped give me a rounded level of experience. Career-wise, my aspirations aren't linked to seniority; it's just really important to me to be able to come to work and be challenged by a role where I can truly make a difference – this could be at my current level or a more senior one.

"With regards to moving up to the next level, my areas of development are commerciality and growing my experience and exposure to other cultures.

"I believe that in the future, HR as a profession needs to focus less on the obsession with being all-round, commercial business partners and be confident enough to really leverage the expertise we have in people matters, like identifying and developing talent, and supporting and leading through change. For instance, when I look at our finance colleagues, they are very clear in what they are there to achieve and are widely considered to be experts in a well-defined field.

"What's stopping HRDs from becoming CEOs? For me, no one can stand up and give a clear and confident North Star for HR. Until we're really clear and confident about the value we add, we'll not have the same credibility as other functions. Also, the certified qualifications held by those in the HR world don't carry the same credibility as those held by someone in finance, which lessens their professional impact. Aligned to this is a concern that I get better professional development from doing what I do on the job than what I get from being a member of the CIPD."

A great story from Ben, and I'm sure that he will go on to better and greater things in his career.

I wanted to give you another perspective which I think you will find really interesting. Here's Andrew's story following my interview with him:

Andrew Martin (Head of HR Business Partners – Airbus Industrial)

"My main vocation of choice at school was journalism as I really enjoyed writing and as a result studied English Language and Literature. During this time, I became aware of 'Personnel' as they called it back then, not via the classic school careers office route but simply through a friend's father who worked as a recruitment headhunter.

"Following school, I went to university to study psychology. I wasn't necessarily considering a career as a psychologist, it was more that the subject field was very people-centric and I had an emerging interest in what we now refer to as 'Emotional Intelligence'.

"It was while I was at university that British Aerospace (now Airbus) came to my attention via the 'milkround', ie where employers come into universities looking to attract the brightest talent to work for them. I applied to their graduate programme, selecting Human Resources as my preferred function, and was offered a position in October 1999.

"I've remained at Airbus ever since, enjoying a number of positions both in HR and in operational functions. My current role sees me located at the Company HQ in Toulouse, working as a Senior Transnational HR Business Partner. I have a team of around 100 HR professionals responsible for supporting the full, global industrial perimeter of Airbus (11 plants, comprising circa 25,000 employees).

"My career with Airbus to date has flexed between Human Resources and General Operational Management. In 2005, I took my first step out of HR to become Senior Manager for an Airbus production unit before returning to HR as Head of HR for Airbus' largest plant. Prior to taking up my current position, I spent the period between 2013 and mid-2017 as Head of Plant for our facility in Filton, Bristol, UK.

"In terms of membership of professional bodies, I did my Associate Member Accreditation with the CIPD but I haven't maintained it. In Europe, the CIPD qualification does not really carry any significance, although on a personal level it's something I wish I had secured. In recognition of my contribution to the aerospace industry, and mainly for my operational roles, the Royal Aeronautical Society has made me an Honorary Fellow.

"With regards to future career aspirations, I remain open minded. In most businesses, and certainly at Airbus, HR has a well-earned and privileged seat at the top table.

This means you are in a position to influence the strategy and performance of the business, and at the same time it provides a lot of breadth about the overall landscape of the company, the bigger picture.

"Nonetheless, HR remains today a support function and its contribution – whilst a critical enabler to the business results – is different from the level of accountability I have enjoyed when in a more operational environment. I enjoy equally the hands-on leadership jobs that allow me to step out of a broader support function role and go deeper into an area of the business where the buck truly stops with me. Maybe I'm destined to rotate between these two worlds!

"I am not sure that I would like to be a CEO of a big company, but I can see myself as the CEO of a small to medium enterprise. Why not a bigger company? Firstly, the inevitable corporate politics of large companies is something I am still learning to navigate (and tolerate!) Secondly, I perceive the profiles of colleagues who have proven track records in commercial, financial and/or business transformation domains as better qualified than me and would therefore be more credible candidates for a CEO-level appointment.

"On a more general level, for HR professionals to succeed as future CEOs, we have to identify career paths to take our leaders in and out of the function so that they can appreciate aspects such as political environments, external factors, programme management, full operational and financial accountability etc. At the moment CFOs and COOs (Chief Operating Officers) are at the front of that queue. Most people in HR take their time to work their way up the ladder within HR, which means that by the time they get there they are comfortable and are less inclined to make a switch. I'm not aware of anyone in my network who has made the leap from HRD to CEO, although I do know of one person who could have - being a purist CHRO - but for whatever reason decided not to.

"For HR to change, we have to focus more on people culture and strategy than simply being a "service provider". Culture eats strategy for breakfast, so priority must centre around the values and behaviours in an organisation. HR has a massive role to play as a change agent. "How" things are done is increasingly the differentiator when it comes to attracting and retaining talent. Is HR leading the charge to ensure companies are better prepared for tomorrow? What skills and competencies are needed – and where – now and in the future to remain competitive? How do we create agile HR policies, processes and systems in this new digital world? Who are the leaders for tomorrow and how do we make them ready to lead a workplace generation that is radically different from what we've seen before?

"The list of challenges and opportunities for HR to make a positive contribution is lengthy. However, at the same time, a balance is needed. HR needs to be careful not to walk away from some of its core duties. Basic contractual matters, compensation and benefits, policy creation, social/industrial relations and many others must remain a key responsibility of HR. If we continue to offload these basic fundamentals to third parties or directly onto the shoulders of employees and managers, we are, in essence, questioning the need for HR at all."

Some really great thoughts from Andrew that we will come back to in later chapters. I've no doubt from my conversation with Andrew, that he will one day be that CEO.

Person D – The Manager who moves sideways into HR because of x, y or z

If you refer back to Chapter 1, this seems to be the increasingly common way that people move into HR and become an HRD. Is this approach always right for the organisation, or for the individual and more importantly, for the reputation of HR?

Person E – The HR Apprentice (mostly seen only in the UK)

Welcome to the new kid on the block. This route into HR has become more apparent in the last few years as young adults decide that full-time education is not the only way to go. It's potentially a longer route to becoming an HRD, but the good news is that it combines working for a company, studying via day-release or night school, and being paid at the same time. It also teaches you something which you cannot get from college or university: real tangible experience rather than the schooled and educated way of looking at HR.

A colleague of mine who's studying for his CIPD qualifications summed this up really well the other day when he made the following statement:

"It's ironic that what you learn from the book is only one way of putting things into practice. It's like when you pass your driving test, you really don't know how to drive until you take those 'L' plates off!"

Never a truer word said!

Person F – There may be others - let me know if I missed any out!

Of course, there is a lot of generalisation going on here, especially for Persons B to E, but I hope you get the gist of the picture I'm trying to paint.

You may be wondering why I chose to add this chapter to the book and what relevance it has to the aims. If it's not evident right now, then let me give you my view on this.

Most people fall into HR and therefore their drive is starting from a very low level. They lack the inspiration of having seen what a great HRD does because it's not relative to their peer group or the people above them who inspire them as they enter the work environment.

As a profession, HR is still playing catch-up against those in the other functions, eg finance, who have staked a claim at the top table, are seen as professionals and the people who you should try to aspire to be. So, HR needs to turn this tide and the current HRDs have a responsibility to get out there and sort this out. Yes, the CIPD, with their 145,000 members around the world, are trying to reverse this trend, but compare this to the ACCA (**13**) where they have 198,000 members and 490,000 students in 178 countries and you start to understand the delta in credibility.

If you remember back to Chapter 1, I asserted that HR is not taken seriously, and HR hasn't moved forward. No surprise then, based on my findings above, that people are, on the whole, "falling" into HR.

At the time of writing this, a great article was published in *The Daily Telegraph* (**15**) which reported that CEO Warren

East of Rolls Royce had brought in a non-HR-background HRD:

"Warren East [...] is attempting to reinvigorate his turnaround of Britain's engineering flagship by putting someone with no direct experience of human resources in charge of managing people within the business.

"Ex-soldier Harry Holt, the president of the FTSE 100 company's nuclear division, will take over the HR role in early 2018. The move is aimed at kick-starting Mr East's drive to make the business more streamlined."

It's really interesting that:

- Warren did not look to bring in an external purist HR Director;

- that he went for someone, as he puts it, who has "no direct experience" of Human Resources and,

- reading between the lines, that he saw this person as a catalyst to, as they put it, "streamlining the business" which invariably means, I guess, people moves and "restructuring".

I wonder, have we lost the human part from Human Resources?

By the way, I did try to connect with Warren and Harry via LinkedIn to try to get their views, but unfortunately, I wasn't successful. It's a great shame as I would have loved to get their insight as to why Harry was selected for the role and more importantly, why a purist HRD was not brought in.

Summary and recap

We started this chapter off looking at how HR Directors come into the role, and the routes they follow. As you can see from the basic research that I captured above, the majority don't start their work career in HR, but often "end up" in HR and work their way up to becoming HRDs. We have looked at five great examples of HRDs who landed in HR and successfully worked their way up to the top. I theorised about the other avenues of how people reach the top and left open the door so that you can suggest a few more.

As we did in Chapter 1, let's look back at some of the aims of this book to see how we are doing:

- **Why don't HRDs, Boards and CEOs see the current blind spots?**

It's because nothing is changing and no one in HR is asking the right questions! Aspirationally, people who are going into HR don't see this as a stepping stone into something else.

- **What can HRDs do to bring back parity in the boardroom?**

For me it's much more than just HRDs – it's the whole function and support network that needs to change. HR needs to stand up and be counted if it's ever going to evolve. If you are reading this book, then perhaps you are the catalyst. However, it needs to go deeper than this and we need institutions like the CIPD, colleges and universities to jump on this research. We need to change the way that HR is thought of, otherwise it will never move on.

- **Why HRDs never make the transition to CEO while other Board Members do?**

I think the above chapter has clearly painted that picture as to why. Overlay the rest of the aims with what you have read in this chapter and it's not difficult to see that the number of people landing or falling into HR then correlates to the number of people who actually make the transition to becoming an HRD and a CEO.

A great and current example was given towards the end of this chapter where Rolls Royce hired a leader with no direct experience of HR and allocated them into an HRD role because the CEO wanted to "streamline the business"! I've never met Harry so I've no idea how he will approach this challenge, but it brings me back to what is the greatest asset to any business: generally it's their people. Therefore, the question must be asked as to how Harry will rise to the challenge whilst keeping this fact in mind. Time will no doubt tell.

CHAPTER 3

HOW DO OTHER FUNCTIONS GROW THEIR LEADERS?

In comparison with HR, the shortest answer to that question is: a lot better than HR does for sure. Anecdotally, in my experience, people who make it to the top of their function, whether it's sales, IT or finance, have, on the whole, worked their way up through the ranks.

In addition, consider again the ACCA statistics quoted in Chapter 2 in comparison to those of HR and it can be seen that there is a greater mass going into finance and other professional institutions than into HR. Also, think back to your school days and consider that mathematics has always been there and information technology has gained greater and greater presence in the curriculum; HR on the other hand doesn't really figure at all.

So, let us come back to Chapter 1 where we talked about blind spots. In my opinion, most CEOs tend to come up through the ranks, ie if it's an engineering company, the CEO is likely to have been an engineer, Harald Krüger (**16**) for example, who was CEO of BMW Group, graduated from university with a degree in mechanical engineering.

Likewise, if it's a computer technology company like Apple, the CEO is likely to have been a developer, as in the case of Tim Cook (**17**), although Tim did a BSc in industrial engineering and later an MBA.

Or note the findings of an online article produced by ICAS (https://www.icas.com/ca-today-news/one-in-four-ceos-are-chartered-accountants) (**18**) written by Andrew Harbison (May 2016) which touched on the following research by UK recruitment firm Robert Half in their 2016 survey. The survey looked at what advantage would be had by someone with accountancy experience when going for a CEO role in the FTSE 100:

"Almost one in four (23%) FTSE 100 CEOs are chartered accountants.

"The report indicates that finance experience is continuing to be the most common career trait among the C-suite, with 55% of UK CEOs coming from a financial background.

- *Finance: 55%*

- *Retail and hospitality: 21%*

- *Engineering: 15%*

- *Marketing: 15%*

- *Technology: 14%*

"This trend is supported by this year's findings where experience within a single industry combined with a foundation in finance is what organisations seek from those taking the helm."

As you can see from the above, there is or was at the time of writing this book, a clear advantage in having a finance background in gaining the top job, or at least, as commented in the article, experience gained within a single industry together with an accountancy background is almost essential. Do you think this is a blind spot of the FTSE 100 or is it an intentional thing which has been set as the blueprint for the role of the CEO? Personally, I think that it is and was totally intentional.

Quick quiz question: can anyone spot where HR stands in those top 5 business functions? Oh dear, I think I've given the game away – it isn't there!

For those reading this book who say the above table is wrong (like me, I might add) I did check it with the team at Robert Half and I was told that the reason why it doesn't add up to 100% is because some of the CEOs may have cross-discipline experience! So, there you go.

By the way, if you do read the full 2016 article, it did go on to say that only six women were listed out of the 100; maybe that's another book waiting to be written.

Incidentally, the 2017 survey which I looked at on the Robert Half website (**19**) gave a thought-provoking perspective on the results. However, when I spoke to the team, they confirmed that they weren't able to recreate the above table with updated figures, but the following quote is interesting as it indicates where things are moving:

"In the last four years, the number of CEOs with a technology background has trebled as businesses prepare to compete in an increasingly digital economy. In 2014, only three CEOs had a background in technology, while today, this number has increased to 11. The majority of CEOs continue to have a background in finance, although this figure has fallen to 43% from 55% last year, the lowest level in three years. Of those CEOs with a financial background, nearly half (19% of the total) are chartered accountants."

Casting your mind back to Chapter 1, it appears that Richard Hill may have been correct when he made his comment about Boards not trusting a new CEO who hadn't come from a CFO background.

Ironically, as I was researching this chapter I found a very apt piece of research by Tim Vine, Vice President, Risk

Management, Dun & Bradstreet (**20**) http://www.dnb.com/perspectives/finance-credit-risk/4-trends-in-role-of-modern-finance-leader.html. Regarding the evolution of finance leaders, two hundred CFOs and Financial Directors from across British enterprise were surveyed in 2017, exploring everything from the roles they performed to the issues that caused them concern. The article paints a picture of how finance leaders are under pressure to move from A to B in their roles.

Here are the four trends that they are facing:

1. Great expectations – the face of finance is changing at a rapid pace.

2. Under pressure – finance leaders are pressured to do more with less.

3. Smarter decisions – finance leaders must fuel growth with data.

4. High risk – finance leaders face the danger of conflicting priorities.

In the foreword of Tim's article, the following statement is noteworthy, so I have added it in bold for effect:

"Occupying a unique role at the heart of the organisation, attuned to the big picture as well as the minutiae of every department, no one else can offer quite the same degree of strategic insight as the finance leader. Little wonder that so many organisations now rely on their financial leaders to help push the business forward."

I did love Tim's comments but if this is how finance is seen in relation to other functions, then maybe this is another blind spot which we have uncovered? You might reach the conclusion that it's not only HR that needs to evaluate its leaders and place in the overall structure of companies and organisations.

I contacted Tim via LinkedIn, and after making a connection, I asked him to comment further on the above quote, however he didn't respond to the following questions:

- Why do you think that no other function has this view?

- Moreover, what's stopping HR and HRDs from having this big picture view of every department?

I'd like to take this opportunity of apologising to Tim if my question was badly phrased, as I mentioned that my first reaction to his comment was that it seemed slightly arrogant.

I do wonder if this view is representative across finance, and moreover, Boards and CEOs in general; if so, then again, is this something else that we must change?

There were some other interesting statistics in the report that I felt I needed to bring out, the reason for which will become evident in the future stages of this book as we look at the evolution of HRness and HR professionals.

1. 53% of finance leaders have experienced "significant" changes in their role.

2. 59% of respondents noted that their role now necessitates greater management of risk and compliance issues.

3. 91% of respondents agreed that their role has become more challenging over the last three years.

4. 50% stress the importance of operational cost-cutting and the need for more efficiency when asked what has driven the evolution of their role.

5. 45% of financial leaders say they struggle with not having a large enough team to do the work at hand.

6. 60% of financial leaders say that their team size has actually decreased over the past few years.

Ironically, I believe the last two points are representative of any support function that is not seen to be adding value to the bottom line.

So, I seem to have locked in, deliberately I guess, to the finance function when looking into this chapter. However, I am conscious of a subtle change in where their CEOs are coming from. IT as a function is starting to come through strongly, especially among the FTSE 100 as noted in my comments about the Robert Half survey and the 2017 statement earlier in this chapter.

With this in mind, I decided to speak to a finance director to find out more about how finance grows its leaders, and this is a snapshot of the interview:

Darren Lees (Finance Director, Imperial Brands UK&I)

"A role in finance and accountancy has always been my ambition. From the age of about 15, during career talks I knew that I wanted to be a qualified accountant, even though my dad was an HR Director at AXA Insurance. I think this is because I had an awareness from my family and friends of the "classic" career paths: doctors, lawyers, accountants etc, and I saw finance as a cornerstone of every business.

"My A-Levels were focused towards a finance career (doing both Maths and Economics) and then I went to Bristol University to study a BSc in Economics and Accounting. This course (i) gave me exposure to the Big 4 accountancy firms via the milkround, but also (ii) gave me exemptions from first year accountancy exams.

"I learned really early on that the Big 4 accounting firms had a proven route to becoming an Associate Chartered Accountant (ACA) accredited with the Institute of Chartered Accountants England and Wales (ICAEW). If you look at most of the FDs in the FTSE 100, I suspect that the majority of them will be connected to the ACA.

"With regards to progressing up the ladder, accountancy has always been a classic career, whereas in my view, if you work hard, you can progress up the ladder and build yourself a solid and rewarding position within any organisation, so it is very flexible across industry and location. That said, in recent years I've seen an increasing number of people coming through the graduate route who demonstrate a view of an 'entitlement to a career' rather than working hard towards gaining it; this is a shift in mindset for me and one which I find increasingly common.

"Being a CEO is an interesting point. In my view, putting a finance director or accountant in the CEO position during times of **instability, rebuild or cost and** cash **focus**, can truly add value because generally they are risk-averse individuals who are able to focus on financial measures with a clear understanding of the many levers which can be deployed to deliver a strategy or plan.

"That said, there may be other times where a more 'unrestricted' entrepreneurial approach would be better suited to the CEO role, for example, tech / startup entities which would lean more towards someone with a sales and marketing background. The aim of the FTSE 100 CEOs is to add value to the shareholders and the City.

"Why HRDs generally do not make the move to CEO is probably due to the fact that HR is often seen as a 'support' function, rather than a 'leading' function, similar to IT. In my view, only when companies and organisations see their people as their key assets and their unique selling points, (and that is recognised by the City as much as by financial delivery and shareholder value creation, which again, is often financially linked), will we see more HR executives taking the CEO role than we do today.

"Examples of such companies with people at the forefront and the impact those resources have on the corresponding brands of those businesses could be Google, Tesla, and our biggest charities."

A really useful perspective from Darren, definitely someone who will go places.

This interview with Darren, along with the data presented earlier, started me thinking about the role played by institutions like the ACA in the way that finance develops its leaders and CEOs. This is what I found when I looked deeper into their website.

ACA website

At first glance, the website looks no different to many others and it's only when you start to delve into the individual tabs that you really start to get the feel that you are surfing a professional organisation.

The very first tab takes you into the world of Learning and Development and you can't help but be drawn into two sub-categories:

- Continuing professional development courses

- Talent development programmes

Let's take a look at what's under each one:

Continuing professional development courses

Let me first explain what this is; if you are a member of an institute, you are supposed to keep your knowledge and skills up to date each year. You should be ensuring that you spend x amount of time doing things like research and undertaking professional training within the discipline.

No surprises that when I looked at this, I said "Wow!" If you are a member of an HR institute, please just go and have a look at its website and see if there is anything like this available to you. I know that when I checked the CIPD's website, it was, in my opinion, a long way away from the ACA's.

I couldn't help myself from digging further into the tabs, including the "Leadership" tab where I came across these two courses, which I for one, would love to see run by someone like the CIPD:

The high-performing Board Director

"More than ever, individual directors must display exemplary standards of integrity, behaviour and governance whilst contributing fully to their Board and committee deliberations and overseeing strong company performance."

To summarise, the ACA's course (and no, I'm not on any commission) outlines a different way of training our finance colleagues by using film and training simulations to enable conversations around the required technical elements, and also the behavioural issues that Boards face.

The course goes on to look at topics like:

- Cyber security

- Unconscious bias (I've seen numerous HR courses on this)

- Commercial risk management

- Effective and ineffective director behaviours

The last one is an area that we consider quite extensively in Chapter 5 where we look at the effective areas.

Of course, there is more, but for me, it's the learning outcomes which prompted me to bring this to your attention:

1. How to handle technical and behavioural issues common to Boards and their committees.

2. How to navigate potential boardroom politics.

3. Understand your own strengths and development needs in areas such as chairing meetings, influencing and collective decision-making.

4. Discover the behaviours required of an exceptional Board Director.

Wouldn't this be an amazing course for HR and HRDs? It's something which I personally would love to see.

The second course that I wanted to highlight is:

Developing a world-class business partnering function

"You want your team to partner the business, challenge effectively and influence decisions. This course will show you how you can turn it around and develop a world-class business partner team."

Simply put, this course looks at what "world-class" actually means. It's pushing the boundary for finance and setting the bar at the level to which they want to attain. This should be a no-brainer for HR, but the research shows that HR is not moving on, and as I've stated before, HR is just turning out more of the same.

But this course does one other thing which I don't see out in HR-land, and that is to provide the principles for developing plans to "transform finance teams from mere accountants to finance business partners."

Let's quickly look at the learning outcomes of the course and please, again, decide for yourself if this is something that HR needs. I, for one, believe that it is.

Learning outcomes:

1. What world-class finance business partnering looks like and how to communicate it.

2. The finance business partner maturity model and how to use it.

3. How to structure your team and their priorities to free-up time to partner.

4. How to anchor the change with a simple data-to-insight model.

5. The critical skills and capabilities to recruit for or develop internally.

6. The three key interview questions to uncover diamonds.

7. How to embed the change with your team using a coaching approach.

Again, I looked on the CIPD website for anything that would look like the institute setting out the same thing for HR and sadly, I couldn't find that either.

Soldiering on, I wanted to check out the other tab under the heading of Learning and Development mentioned above:

Talent development programmes

Here I was presented with some of the following:

- Women in leadership

- Network of finance leaders

- Mentoring and executive coaching

Like a child in a sweet shop, I could not contain myself, so I almost fell over my mouse mat trying to get to the third one. There I found something truly amazing:

ICAEW Mentoring and Executive Coaching

"Are you new to a finance role and thinking about your next career move? Or do you have a specific business or leadership challenge? If so, ICAEW mentors and coaches can help you. The majority of mentees are in senior leadership or Board level roles and are sponsored by their business."

With my heart in my mouth, I gathered up what hope I had remaining and wandered over to the CIPD website; I will leave it up to you to guess what I found, but let me leave you with this image:

Now I am going to stop at this point, otherwise I will be giving you an HR professional's view of someone else's website and I think I've made my point so let's move on.

However, it would be remiss of me if I didn't share something that I did spot on the ACA website. This was an article from December 2011 by Rachel Short in the *Finance and Management Faculty Magazine* (Issue 194) entitled "'Great' finance leaders should win hearts and minds" (**21**). The aim of the article was to look at the age-old question of what good vs great looks like in relation to finance leaders and how the great ones can be developed:

"What makes a finance leader stand out from the crowd? YSC [formerly Young Samuel Chambers, leadership consultancy] has been researching thousands of organisational leaders and our database tells us that finance professionals have considerable strengths relative to their peers.

"For example, they:

1. *are significantly more analytical, logical and data-rational; and*

2. *can also be stronger at framing organisational strategy and showing sharp commercial judgment and market awareness.*

"Interpersonally, however, they tend to:

1. *be less influential;*

2. *have lower levels of impact; and*

3. *lack insight into how to motivate and inspire as leaders."*

As a result of the above, the article homes in on the area of "lack of influencing skills" which, ironically, can be applied to HR as well. For instance, the article states that most finance leaders first focus on building their technical expertise as they rise through the ranks: not dissimilar to HR. However, where HR and finance then differ is that HR focuses (or should focus) not just on minds, but on hearts too.

One noticeable similarity between finance and HR is that project management skills aren't in the bank of training for either. This is certainly a skill that should be a must for HR as it seeks to align to businesses in general.

Glenn, why did you call this one out? you ask. Well, I wanted to flag that this was one of the first signs that I've seen where finance (in my view) actually wants to be more like HR. After all, isn't this the human part of what we do?

As I was writing this chapter, I found myself fascinated by this and although I could easily go on and on, I trust your intelligence and your ability to see through what I have shown you.

By now you know my style of writing, so let's take another look at the aims of the book to see what this chapter has given you:

Aim No. 1: Why is it almost impossible to move from an HRD to a CEO and what research – or more importantly, lack of research – has driven me to write this book?

The HR function is a million miles behind finance in the race to CEO. It's very clear that until HR's professional institutions change, HR and its directors won't get there so the following need attention:

1. A clear direction (North Star) needs to be set, together with a view on what HR should be in the 21st century, by organisations like the CIPD.

2. Professional training must be provided, as finance does, to raise the bar and standards of our HR leaders.

Let me remind you of Ben Worthington's comments in Chapter 2, just to reinforce the point:

In Ben's opinion, HR needs to focus less on being all-round commercial business partners, but should really leverage the expertise they have in people matters, developing talent, and supporting and leading through change.

He also feels that the professional impact of HR is lessened as the certified qualifications held by those in the HR world don't carry the same credibility as those held by those in finance. Moreover, until they are really clear about the value they add, HR will never have the same credibility.

Ben commented that he feels he gets better professional development from learning "on the job" than he gets from being a member of the CIPD.

Aim No. 2: To set out what HRDs can do to bring them back parity in the boardroom.

It might be too late for the HRDs of today to do this, but the clues have emerged in this chapter with regards to:

1. Raising the professional bar.

2. Developing skills which HRDs lack around taking informed decisions based on data; this will enable logical conclusions to be derived to inform any strategic decisions required.

3. Standing tall in the boardroom and using the HRness powers of influence, insight and inspiration.

Aim No. 3: Why HRDs in general never make the transition to CEO whilst Board Members in other functions do.

I don't think I need to spell this out here, do I?

Aim No. 4: Provide HRDs with the behaviours, competencies and skills required to really add value in the boardroom and to step-up.

We covered some here, but I want to focus on these in later chapters, so keep reading.

Aim No. 5: Ultimately, consider what more broadly than HR needs to happen in order to make the jump to becoming a CEO ahead of their peers.

We are making good progress on this as we work through this book and already, we are starting to see clear differences between HR and the finance function for example. As Darren Lees put it, the "classic" careers vs the not so. Also, it's clear that Boards and existing CEOs don't see the value of their people and their USPs even today: worrying but true.

Aim No. 6: Understand why CEOs and Boards don't see HRDs in the CEO succession plan.

Anybody joined the dots on this one yet? I think it's quite simple: I don't think they have ever contemplated it.

Aim No. 7: Why does the above still manifest itself as a consistent theme and why haven't Boards and CEOs realised the impact on those companies, their workforce and more importantly, their bottom line as a result? Why have Boards and CEOs not embraced HRness?

It takes a fair amount of courage to change and my gut feel is that for some, it's easier to stay with the tried-and-tested rather than to go for something different.

Summary and recap

This chapter was all about how other functions grow their leaders, focussing on finance as HR's closest comparator to stress the points that I needed to show you. I make no bones about where my position is here and I repeat that I believe other functions do this much better than HR.

We looked briefly at where the functions and companies are gaining their leaders from and it's clear that HR is nowhere on the list in the FTSE 100 companies; however, our colleagues, especially finance, are. Boy, are we in trouble!

After this, we looked at an article from Tim Vine which gave an insight into where finance see themselves, especially Tim's comment which I will replay:

"Occupying a unique role at the heart of the organisation, attuned to both the big picture as well as the minutiae of every department, no one else can offer quite the same degree of strategic insight as the finance leader. Little wonder that so many organisations now rely on their financial leaders to help push the business forward."

Add to this, Darren's story and comments where he set out how many companies and organisations see people as assets and how HRDs could be the difference.

During this chapter, we looked at the ACA's website to see why the divide between finance and HR is so wide and hopefully, again you have drawn your own conclusions as to why. I implore you to check out your institute's websites and see if they come up to scratch.

We read Rachel Short's article which touched upon how "great" finance leaders should win hearts as well as minds. Her article gave us an insight into where finance is going and where HR needs to evolve.

Lastly, we recapped at a high level on the seven aims to pull out some thoughts as we build a case through the book.

I trust at this point you are still with me as we journey on to the next chapter where we look at Fixed vs Growth Mindset.

CHAPTER 4

FIXED VS
GROWTH MINDSET

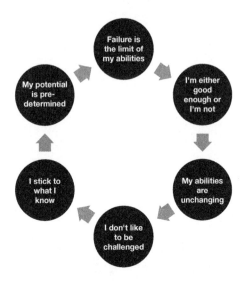

FIXED MINDSET

GROWTH MINDSET

As a visual person, I really love to use pictures. For me the use of pictures and words together invoke the feelings which now I hope will help you to understand this chapter in greater depth.

My first academic research into "Fixed vs Growth Mindset" came from Matthew Syed's book *Black Box Thinking* (**22**) p272. This centred on an experiment that Jason Moser conducted which led to the birth of the growth mindset theory which was later taken further by Carol Dweck. Essentially, the experiment looked at two distinct types of brain signals; one was called "Error Related Negativity" (ERN) (an involuntary brain reaction to making a mistake) and the other "Error Positivity" (Pe) which comes from a different part of the brain when we focus on our mistakes. Still with me? Boy, would my biology teacher be impressed with me now! Moser goes on to say that when the two signals are fired off, if the ERN is larger and the Pe remains stable then the person learns from the mistake.

For the experiment, Moser divided the test group into two by virtue of a pre-completed survey and the following are the results of the experiment:

"People with a fixed mindset tend to believe that their basic qualities, like their intelligence or talent, are largely fixed traits. They strongly agree with statements like 'You have a certain amount of intelligence, and you can't really do much to change it.

"People with a growth mindset, on the other hand, tend to believe that their most basic abilities can be developed through hard work. They do not think that innate intelligence is irrelevant but believe that they can become smarter through persistence and dedication. As a

group, they tend to disagree with statements such as 'your intelligence is something about you that you can't change very much'."

So, I started to contemplate whether this is part of the problem that is blocking HRness and HRDs from making the move forward? After a few paragraphs like that you must be wondering where Glenn is going with this line of thought, and so here you go.

Which mindset do you think existing Boards and CEOs are in when it comes to HRDs being able to make the move to CEO; fixed or growth?

Take this a stage further and ask where HR is when it considers its place in the Boardroom: fixed or growth mindset?

Ask yourself: where are HRDs in their aspirations of being the next CEO: fixed or growth?

One last one: of the companies that are out there, how many look at their employees as an area of growth rather than focussing on their products as being the main benefit to their bottom line: fixed or growth?

I am going to go out on a limb here and guess that the majority of you will answer the above questions with 'Fixed!' – but I could be wrong.

Earlier in the chapter, I mentioned that Carol Dweck took this research a stage further and there's a really great picture showing how Carol differentiates the fixed and the growth mindsets (https://www.pinterest.co.uk/pin/334744184782113947/).

To bring this to life, I thought it might be good if we looked at each element of Carol's brain picture through:

- the eyes of CEOs and Boards on their view of HRDs becoming the next CEO

- the eyes of HRDs and HR

In short, a fixed mindset believes that intelligence is static while a growth mindset believes that intelligence can be developed.

Fixed – leads to a desire to look smart and therefore a tendency to (I will leave it to you to fill in the blanks!).

Growth – leads to a desire to learn and therefore a tendency to create a culture of it's okay to make mistakes as long as you take a learning from them. In other words, it allows innovation and a safe environment where you as an individual are not chastised for trying something different.

1. CEOs and Boards

On reviewing some of the research in Chapter 1, my belief is that CEOs and Boards see their HRDs as not of the calibre that is able to deliver in the "top job" unless they have previously been in a finance or mainstream role within the company, like manufacturing, sales or finance. Therefore, my sense is that they have a fixed mindset and believe that HR's intelligence is static!

1. HRDs and HR

Sweeping statement coming up: I conclude that most of the purist HRDs and those in HR are also in the "fixed" camp and have been happy to accept their roles in the company pushing the same stuff every day without looking at the big picture.

Add to this the supporting HR institutes and you end up in a place which means that the "human" element of HR has simply slipped out of the picture. If you get a chance to read Lucy Adams' book *Disruptive HR*, please do. I leave it up to you to judge how far you agree with Lucy but for me, she is a great example of someone with a growth mindset who is starting to push the "no more, same old, same old" approach.

Challenges:

Fixed mindset – avoids challenges

Growth mindset – embraces challenges

2. CEOs and Boards

Most tend to avoid challenges and as we have seen in the first chapters, the tried-and-tested seems to be the preferred course of action. Again, I would put this group into the fixed mindset category as it's believed that the City would never put someone with an HR background into a CEO role unless they are tried-and-tested.

However, I believe that there are enough tried and tested HRDs out there who would completely break the CEO mould. If you don't believe me, ask yourself the question: in times of recession, how many companies cut back successfully without damaging their brand and to the detriment of their employees? My experience tells me that these are in the minority.

2. HRDs and HR

I may have already answered this for you but as General Colin Powell once said, **"tell them once, tell them again and, oh yes, tell them once more."** HRDs and HR have forgotten to challenge themselves; if you look at the CIPD training offered, they are regurgitating the same old stuff from ten or twenty years ago, and people who attend their courses are fed the same old tried and tested ways.

I suppose it's like when you learn to drive; you don't really drive properly until you've passed your test. But come on, it's time to move on guys! This current mindset is not moving us forward and, as Ben said in Chapter 2, we don't have a North Star for HR, so guess what? We carry on doing what we've always done and there is little new thought coming through to jet-propel HR forward. It's time for HRDs and HR to *embrace* change instead of avoiding it. If we don't, then the robots (which everyone is talking about) will absolutely take over HR – or maybe they already have!

Obstacles:

Fixed mindset – gets defensive or gives up easily

Growth mindset – persists in the face of setbacks

3. CEOs and Boards

Who was it that coined the phrase "the path of least resistance?" I think this sums up the behaviour of most CEOs and Boards when looking for the next CEO and to be honest, I can kind of see why they have this fixed behaviour. Can you imagine the response from the City if, for example, the next CEO for Glencore International (FTSE 100 company), instead of Ivan Glasenberg (who incidentally studied accountancy and commerce at university) was an HR purist? Why not? I ask.

3. HRD and HR

In my experience, I find that HRDs and HR tend to be defensive about what they do, probably because HRness is always seen as a non-value-add to companies. Also, may I bring you back to Patrick Tom's comment in Chapter 1 where he talked about "HR's victim mentality" and why it's unfair that HR is not seen as a value-add. HRDs and HR need to stand up and be counted instead of giving up easily. Until HRness is seen as a critical component of organisations and HR moves away from the victim mentality, this fixed mindset will sadly continue.

Effort:

> Fixed mindset – sees effort as fruitless or worse

> Growth mindset – sees effort as the path to mastery

4. CEOs and Boards

My belief is that the blueprint for being a CEO is one that cannot be changed without real effort and I question whether the Boards and existing CEOs have the appetite to change. If an HRD has the right level of skills, behaviours and tools, then why not? Is it just too much effort for Boards to drag this fixed mindset away from the accepted norm and, as Carol says in her picture, is it just fruitless or pointless? Could you imagine the potential benefit of a leading HRD being a FTSE 100 CEO? I can.

4. HRD and HR

To defend my fellow HR professionals, I don't believe that it's a question of effort at all; my belief is that it's just the fact that HRDs don't see the role of CEO as being a career path for them, unless it's aligned to a company that specialises in HR, like a coaching or recruitment company.

So, let me plant the seed for my colleagues out there around the world: could you be the one to buck the trend here, expend the effort and take the path to master the role of CEO?

Criticism:

Fixed mindset – ignores useful negative feedback

Growth mindset – learn from criticism

5. CEOs and Boards

When I contemplated this one, I genuinely wasn't sure about my feelings but, as I thought about it, I considered the possibility that some Boards have tried to put HRDs in a CEO position and they may have reacted to the criticism they received. That said, coming back to companies and organisations seeing people as their best assets, this tells me that they are on the "fixed" side – ignoring useful negative feedback. I sincerely hope that this doesn't continue.

5. HRD and HR

With regard to HRDs and HR learning from criticism, you can probably guess immediately what I am going to write next. No surprises, and by now, you are getting closer and closer to my psyche (sorry!) I believe that HR absolutely 100% ignores useful negative feedback; if it didn't then I would not be writing a book about the state of HR and why HRDs don't make the move to become CEOs.

Success of Others:

Fixed mindset – feels threatened by the success of others

Growth mindset – final lessons and inspiration in the success of others

6. CEOs and Boards

My gut feel is that CEOs and Boards are oblivious to the lessons of other companies and organisations with regard to changing the CEO blueprint. There is no visible trend to make changes at the top nor do anything different. Unless of course, you count the rise of technology as more and more comes online.

Remember the research I shared with you which stated that in the FTSE 100, not one of the CEOs came from an HR background. Perhaps in saying this I've just hit the nail on the head and it's simply down to the fact that there's been no successes to model this on. Therefore, unfortunately this falls into the "fixed" camp.

6. HRD and HR

I was really puzzled on this part as there are clear examples of where HRDs have become CEOs, but I just don't get why more and more HRDs haven't made the move, or at least pushed the envelope to test it. Perhaps it's just lethargy or a lack of direction again. What do you think?

Conclusions:

> Fixed mindset – may plateau early and achieve less than their full potential

> Growth mindset – may reach ever-higher levels of achievement

7. CEOs and Boards

I am hoping that this very interesting and insightful chapter has opened your eyes to where I think CEOs and Boards are. However, if they are still tightly shut or you are choosing to look away, let me give you my view.

I'll use the analogy of the football manager who is given a few matches to turn things around for the team struggling at the bottom of the league. If results are not immediate, they are quickly released. The only difference is that the manager may be given a sizeable pay-out to persuade him to give up the task and leave.

I firmly believe, and I would go so far as to say that I have evidence, that Boards and existing CEOs don't see HRDs as being the answer. Moreover, when purist HRDs have been given a chance, I don't believe that they have been given long enough to turn things around. That said, we have already talked about those CEOs who have been successful but were not out-and-out purist HRDs. Remember Mary Barra who was Vice President of Global HR for three years and went on to become Chairman and CEO of General Motors.

7.   HRDs and HR

No surprises that my view of HRDs and HR puts them fully in the camp of being in the "fixed" section when looking at the overall result. HRDs and HR are punching well below their ability, and, given the sense of lethargy, I don't see this changing very soon.

Looking to the future my belief is that the CEO's of the future do need experience in HR as a function for a period of time (there is evidence that where this happens there is a tangible result). In addition, maybe some HR managers or directors as a result of reading this book will be inspired to reach those higher levels of achievement that is well within them. However, this relies heavily on companies having the foresight (growth mindset) and courage to allow HR professionals to grow and learn outside of HR.

Your thoughts after reading this chapter?

I appreciate that I may have gone on and on, but I truly felt that the Fixed vs Growth Mindset theory is really important; it is for me as it's deeply rooted in who I am as a person. Moreover, if we are to make a difference (and I sincerely hope we are) that after reading and digesting this book, it is essential for HR to start doing this right now.

So, as we sign off this chapter, why not look at the table below and challenge yourself to see where you land? Before you do that though, please keep this in mind: most people will instantly say they are firmly on the growth mindset side, but I ask you to seek 360-degree feedback to truly validate where you are. If you recall, we started this book talking about blind spots, so this may be yours.

Leaders with Fixed Mindset	Leaders with Growth Mindset
Like to use their strengths	Surround themselves with a strong team
Focus on achieving fast and dramatic results	Work towards sustainable results
Like to 'keep people on their toes'	Coach and empower people
Have a strong sense of entitlement	Express gratitude
Are happy to fire those who challenge them	Are tough but compassionate
Blame others if their reputations are at risk	Use 'we' rather than 'I'
Surround themselves with 'flatterers'	Encourage learning from mistakes
Like to be seen as the hero	Show humility
Are controlling	Seek out new ideas and opinions
Are easily bored	Don't give up

Summary and recap

I am really not going to summarise too much on this chapter as I believe by now you are totally on the same page as me. If not, then at least I've made you consider another view by introducing the Fixed vs Growth Mindset thinking.

The chapter introduced a few aspects from Matthew Syed's book *Black Box Thinking* which I recommend as a really good read. Yes, a lot of it is common sense, but it's really good common sense. This chapter talked about the research that Moser did and gave some great examples of fixed vs growth mindset.

After this I framed the following questions for you:

1. Which mindset do you think existing Boards and CEOs are in when it comes to HRDs being able to make the move to CEO: fixed or growth?

2. Take this a stage further and ask where HR is when it considers its place in the universe we call Boards: fixed or growth?

3. Ask yourself where are HRDs in their aspirations of being the next CEO: fixed or growth?

4. And finally, of the companies that are out there, how many look at their employees as areas of growth vs focussing/fixating on their products as being their main benefit to their bottom line; fixed or growth I ask you?

To enable your thinking around the above four questions, we stepped through Carol Dweck's brain picture and it was clear that the majority of answers came back to being "fixed" rather than "growth"!

So, to summarise: now we know the problems, who's prepared to do something about it?

Is it you, Mr or Mrs Reader, CEO; is it you, Mr or Mrs Board Member, or Mr or Mrs HR Director; is it you, Professor Reader, or Mr or Mrs School or College Head? Or is it your Mum or Dad?

We touched on where you are as the reader of this book and we set you a challenge to see where you fit. Are you part of the problem or part of the solution?

As you read through the rest of this book, keep in mind the aims as listed in Chapter 1 and I hope that this is evolving your thinking and you are making changes already.

CHAPTER 5

BEHAVIOURS OF THE GREAT CEOS

Still with me? I really hope so.

When I decided to put this chapter in the book I knew that the research might be difficult to get hold of, but I accepted the challenge in an effort to ensure that we pull out what it is that great CEOs do, in order to show what's missing from HR and HRDs' kit bags. Why? I hear you say. Well, in coaching, one of the things that is impressed upon you is to search out those people that really do things well, and once you find them, model yourself on them. Now whilst I recognise that might not always work because your view on someone who does something very well might be different from another's, however, you get the point yes?

Before we press ahead let's just make sure that we are all on the same page regarding the definition of "behaviour" as defined by the online Oxford dictionary (**23**):

Behaviour: The way in which one **acts** or **conducts** oneself, especially towards **others**.

1.   *'he will vouch for her good behaviour'*

2.   *'his insulting behaviour towards me'*

3.   *[as modifier] 'behaviour patterns'*

4.   *[count noun] 'management is a set of techniques and behaviours for getting things done'*

So now we are all on the same page, let's look at what my research found.

The first online article that I found was published by McKinsey and was entitled "What makes a CEO exceptional?" (**24**) written by Michael Birshan, Thomas

Meakin and Kurt Strovink. For those data geeks out there, Michael and his colleagues looked at those CEOs who were defined as the very top performers out of roughly 600 CEOs at Standard & Poor's (S&P) 500 companies between 2004 and 2014. Again, to make sure I am fulfilling your need for clarity the S&P 500 according to Wikipedia (**25**) is:

"The Standard & Poor's 500, often abbreviated as the S&P 500, or just the S&P, is an American stock market index based on the market capitalizations of 500 large companies having common stock listed on the NYSE or NASDAQ."

The Outsider's Edge (**24**):

"On average, CEOs who are hired externally tend to pull more strategic levers than those who come from within and outperform their internal counterparts."

If you recall, earlier in the book we talked about the traditional CEO recruitment blueprint. In the research from Michael and colleagues, they called out that CEOs are twice as likely to have been recruited from outside of the company as from within. However, the main point here was around being able to take an outsider's view, therefore, the behaviour we are looking at here is the ability to take an **impartial and focused view** as a result of being new.

I hear you already saying as you read this chapter, so what has this got to do with behaviour? Summing up what I have taken from the article, I would say that it is referring to **objectivity and influence**.

New CEOs are hired fairly evenly from both internal and external routes, but it's the external CEO coming in without any emotional baggage or preconceptions who breathes new life into the role. They deal solely with the facts – **objectivity** - and they are then able to move the company forward using their **influence** - the next big factor.

What's missing from HR and HRDs' kit bags?

Objectivity – HR and HRDs today have systems in place that are driving a huge amount of data, (whether it's the right data is another question), but how is it being used? My view is that we are not objective in how we work. It does come back to the previous chapter insomuch as we are just going along with the wave instead of getting in front of it.

Ask yourself what is being done with the data and then ask yourself: how much **influence** do HR and HRDs have in their organisations? My view is that it's probably up to a certain level but nowhere near where it needs to be. The best CEOs that I have seen have been able to come into a company, understand it "warts and all", use the data really well and make informed changes quickly from several data points. In addition, they form credible business relationships quickly by being able to understand how that business ticks.

Do you remember back in Chapter 1 when we looked at where HR spends most of its time? Well, just to recap: at the maximum it was 28% on strategic business partnering. How influential are you?

By the way, did you know that the CIPD offer a two-day course on "The Art of Influencing" which looks to be pretty good? Here's an outline of the course to whet your appetite:

"Designed to offer participants a modern, holistic approach to the complex, exciting field of face-to-face influencing. This course encourages participants to develop a keen understanding and curiosity for the art form, which brings 21st century theory to life, demystifying its complexities and making them accessible to all."

The next part of Michael *et al*'s article referred to:

Strategic actions: *"In our sample as a whole, CEOs joining low-performing companies derived the biggest benefits from conducting a strategic review."*

Essentially, the article stated that almost immediately the new CEO took their post, they initiated a strategic review. On the back of this, the top-performing CEOs enacted changes. It's not surprising that once again, one of those actions listed was "cutting costs in the lower parts of the company" – usually employees.

What's missing from HR and HRDs' kit bags?

I wish that books in the future could be bi-directional in how they work; wouldn't it be amazing if, when you read a book, you had access to the author?

Anyway, I digress. It seems to me that this can be answered in two parts:

1.   The ability to act strategically through a total-company lens.

2. The ability to do something different instead of implementing cost-reduction programmes that are a short-term fix but do nothing for your people and the morale of a company.

Let's look at point 1 first. From my point of view, I don't believe that HR or HRDs do look strategically at the organisation to pre-empt or advise CEOs of what to do next. In my opinion, they are, on the whole, a bystander in any strategic changes that happen, which are often discussed only by the CEO and the CFO or Board. Therefore, HR and HRDs need to gain that ability to look critically at their companies and come up with 21st century options that fit our world.

A great example of this is the ongoing debate about Artificial Intelligence and the impact of robotics over the next 20 to 30 years. What is HR's role in dealing with this and how is HR leading the way and managing employees' concerns? If you get the chance to listen to the following podcast from the CIPD, they touch on this as part of their look-ahead for 2018 (**26**), but what is HR actually doing about it? **https://www.cipd.co.uk/podcasts/look-ahead-2018**

Now for point 2. I concede that there is a time and a place for cost-reduction programmes but it's *how* you do it which gives you the true positive or negative outcome. HR and HRDs should be straight into this conversation by leading the way on ideas which meet the needs of the business, but guide and deliver any changes in a professional and human way.

All too often, you hear about companies who push the button to cut costs but damage their overall brand reputation in the process: this must be something that HR takes forward, truly adding value at the CEO level. This isn't missing from the kitbag of HR or HRDs, but, for whatever reason, and maybe it's back to the influencing point, the advice and words are not reaching where they need to be.

The third element of Michael's research called out:

Organisational balance or redesign: *"Those among our sample of exceptional CEOs, though, were less likely than the average CEO to undertake organisational redesign or management team reshuffles in the first two years in office."*

Whilst organisational balance and redesign is a big tool to the high-performing CEOs in being able to effect a change of strategy, the key message that came out of this was "patience". But also, having the right people around you is crucial for the success of any new CEO.

What's missing from HR and HRDs' kit bags?

This should be a no-brainer for HR and HRDs to answer; however, if you are in HR, let me challenge you by asking the question, "Is your HR function set up with the right performing people and if not, what are you doing about it?"

One thing that was clear from Michael's research and commentary was that modelling the behaviours of the exceptional CEOs is a must.

This was a good start in highlighting behaviours of great CEOs. However, I just felt that there was more than this, so my research turned up this article from the *Harvard Business Review* (**27**) (May 2017) written by Elena Lytkina Botelho, Kim Rosenkoetter Powell, Stephen Kincaid and Dina Wang, which talked about "What sets successful CEOs apart".

The piece that Elena *et al* generated highlighted the impact and the costs involved when CEOs leave companies (a 2014 PwC study estimated $112 billion in lost market value annually) and also why companies, when it comes to having the right CEOs, are getting things wrong.

If you recall earlier in the book, we looked at the traditional CEO blueprint, and the article that I refer to also comments about the disconnect between what Boards think and the stereotyping that goes on. I totally recommend that you look at this great article as you will get far more from it than I can relay here.

So, let's look at the main reason why we brought this research to light and home in on the four behaviours identified in Elena's work. First, let me share with you a quote from the article:

"But our most important discovery was that successful chief executives tend to demonstrate four specific behaviours that prove critical to their performance. We also found that when Boards focus on those behaviours in their selection and development processes, they significantly increase their chances of hiring the right CEO."

The four behaviours:

1. Deciding with speed and conviction

2. Engaging for impact

3. Adapting proactively

4. Delivering reliably

1. Deciding with Speed and Conviction

"Good CEOs realise that a wrong decision may be better than no decision at all."

To summarise this section of the article, it really does come down to the above quote. There's no surprise that Elena *et al* stated that they found that CEOs who were decisive in decision-making were twelve times more likely to be high performers.

What's missing from HR and HRDs' kit bags?

For those people in HR or those people who are HRDs are reading this book, what did you take from this behaviour? When I look back at the HRDs who I've had the pleasure of working with, my view is that I would see this as a 50/50 split i.e. I have seen some very decisive HRDs who know where they want the People Strategy to go and conversely and sadly some HRDs who just go with the flow. I know you are going to say that I am sitting on the fence, but this has been my reality to date. What's your reality? All too often, HR looks for consensus at the top table but lack of conviction means that change is slow and often based on the old "safe" ways of doing things.

2. Engaging for Impact

"We found that strong performers balance keen insight into their stakeholders' priorities with an unrelenting focus on delivering business results."

In summary, the article suggests that CEOs who are from top to bottom and back again engaging within companies ie they actively take the time to talk to people at all levels and are physically visible eg take the time to visit stores, factories etc and are the ones that are most successful when making changes or explaining the strategy. A great example of this for me was Justin King, the former CEO of the UK company, Sainsbury's. I remember that during his tenure, Justin really made a difference to the company's direction of travel and profitability and was often seen in the stores around the UK leading and explaining what he was doing and why.

In addition, the behaviour of being able to seek and listen to advice and guidance is very different to that of seeking consensus. Another key element that comes out in the article is the ability to exude confidence throughout the company; i.e. the confidence that their team, the Board and the company will be successful even though tough decisions will have to be made. Let me be clear – this is confidence and not arrogance.

What's missing from HR and HRDs kit bags?

You would think that HRDs and people in HR should be good at this behaviour. After all, we are all about people, and engaging people and stakeholder management should be exactly what we are good at, right?

Again, I have seen some really good HRDs doing this in the past, so I know HR people can do it. Part of this behaviour is linked absolutely to influencing which ironically, we touched on before, so here we have more evidence of this being seen as a pre-requisite for our HR CEOs of the future.

In addition to the above, HR really does get stuck in "consensus" mode, when in reality, as "subject matter experts", we should be able to listen, understand and then make decisions. But for whatever reason, this is something that HR needs to change because it's not what is happening at Board level. This comes back once again to the credibility of HR in the boardroom and in general. Remember the old quote from Chapter 1 that HR is seen as "purely an admin function"! Now, I am not asking HR to suddenly become a bulldozer and just rail-road things through, but we do need to see a step change and embrace this behaviour.

3. Adapting Proactively

"For evidence of how important it is for businesses and leaders to adjust to a rapidly changing environment, we need look no further than the aftermath of Brexit and the recent U.S. presidential election. Our analysis shows that CEOs who excel at adapting are 6.7 times more likely to succeed." (27)

In short, this behaviour is all about the focus of the CEO and their ability to adapt quickly to the environment i.e. business, climate and commercial factors. The statistic that jumped out at me from the above article was that the top-performing CEOs focused as much as 50% of their time on the consideration of the long-term future of the company. Ask yourself, as a current HRD, how much time you spend doing this with your CEO.

If you recall back in Chapter 1, Richard Hill mentioned the word "curious" when discussing the behaviours required and ironically this came out in the research too. It was said that pro-active CEOs look at external sources, trends and data to see things happening before others do. So again, another question for the HRDs out there, how curious are you when it comes to trends, data and developing thought, and how often do you move before others in HR?

Finally, it was nice to see the article referencing "growth mindset", especially in the realm of improvement and learning.

What's missing from HR and HRDs' kit bags?

Aha! I found some recent research that references Brexit (Britain's proposed exit from the European Union), Donald Trump's election as US President and "growth mindset": does that mean I win a prize or have I just been really lucky in pulling this book together?

Anyway, enough of that, I hear you say. We have already covered in previous chapters HR's inability to adapt to the 21st century. We also touched on my thoughts about where HR and HRDs are in the growth mindset stakes so, what have we not covered which is highlighted here?

For me, the element we have not talked about is that 50/50 split regarding what is now and what will be the future, ie the ability to look at the long term, whether it's on your own or with your current CEO. How many people in HR do you see doing this and how often is this left to our colleagues in finance, who invariably, will look at it through the commercial lens?

I ask you, as HR professionals, to challenge yourselves once again when answering the questions above, especially the strategic items and the questions relating to bringing in innovation before anyone else.

4. Delivering Reliably

"Mundane as it may sound, the ability to reliably produce results was possibly the most powerful of the four essential CEO behaviours."

Simply put, this is "doing what you said you would do and when you said you would do it!" This behaviour means that if you do this well, then you build up credibility in the area of delivery. No surprises when the research by Elena *et al* turned out a "94% score for those CEO candidates who followed through in their commitments"!

Of course, to deliver reliably you do need to ensure that you have the right team, the right data or metrics from multiple points, the right project management skills, ie planning and control, and of course, my all-time favourite, local and global accountability.

What's missing from HR and HRDs kit bags?

Reliability: actually, I don't think this is missing from HR or HRDs' kit bags at all; instead I think it's because HR never gets the credit for this element of what we do. Therefore, instead of going on about this, HR and HRDs need to advertise and promote their reliability a lot more than they do currently, but please do take a moment to look at whether you and your own HR team, and your HRD, do deliver reliably?

This behaviour is also closely linked to the growth mindset element which we touched on in Chapter 4. Also, it's interesting to me that discipline is also called out in the article, ie the discipline of having project management skills, regular meetings, using data and metrics to inform decisions etc.

Lastly, it seems that this behaviour is also linked to adapting insomuch that CEOs need to have the right people around them to enable them to move forward. HR needs to really look in the mirror and raise this bar high; we need to take some of our own medicine, ie we preach to our employees that performance is key, but we forget to apply the same lens to our teams; it's time to act.

I really did enjoy reading the article by Elena *et al* and if you get the chance, please do look at the conclusion.

I am hoping that you really found this chapter useful, and that once again, it has opened your eyes a little more. Or at least it's made you think. Before we close this chapter, I wanted to bring in a final piece of information which comes from an article written by Stephanie Chung (28) called *10 Personality Traits Successful CEOs Share* to ensure that I have given you at least three data points of reference.

Some of the following we have already covered, so rather than bore you with more detailed information, here's the top line data for you:

1. **Ability to learn from the past** – we touched on this during Chapter 4 discussing growth mindset, so nothing new to add.

2. **Strong communication skills** – we have already discussed this in the **engaging** element earlier in this chapter so nothing additional here.

3. **Building relationships** – linked to the **engaging** part in this chapter.

4. **Realistic optimism** – another one linked to **engaging for impact**.

5. **Understanding** – aha: a new one. I knew if I kept going I would eventually cover off something else, so let's see what Stephanie says about this trait:

"A CEO must be understanding of matters in and out of the workplace. Employees are people with lives outside of work, and if there's an emergency, a CEO should be understanding and let the employee handle it."

I would be absolutely gobsmacked if anyone in HR got this one wrong. One thing that I think stands HR people out more than others is their Emotional Intelligence. You can write to me if you think I've got this wrong though!

1. **Listening skills** – covered in the Engaging for Impact section above.

2. **Willingness to take calculated risks** – covered in the Deciding with Speed and Conviction section above.

3. **Reading people and adapting to necessary management styles** – partly covered in the Engaging for Impact and Adapting Proactively sections. However, when I read what Stephanie Chung wrote, I had to challenge myself as to whether this was another gap in HR and HRDs' kit bags. So, before I give you my opinion let's read what Stephanie put:

"Not everyone has the same learning style and if you want your company and your employees to succeed, it's important to be able to adapt to the needs of your employees."

So, here are my thoughts: I am not convinced that in HR we do adapt to various needs, since, if we did, then we would be looking at our people as being very different. For example, a one-size-fits-all for training cannot be the best approach. We probably do it because that's the most cost-effective but is it the right approach? Therefore, if we are thinking this way, then this must be one thing that has to change if we ever hope to become the next CEO.

1. **Coaching employees effectively** – another new one so here's Stephanie's view on what this means to her:

"It's your job to give your employees the tools they need to be successful. You must be able to teach and train in a way that inspires your staff to succeed."

Is this missing from HR and HRDs' kit bag? My own personal belief is "yes". We have already talked in previous chapters about how lethargic HR is, so we cannot put our hands on our hearts and say we absolutely do this! Ask yourself the question, do you teach and train in a way that inspires your staff and team?

2. **Thinking outside the box** – linked completely to growth mindset and covered in Chapter 4.

We have spent a lot of time on this chapter so that we can:

*   clearly understand what exceptional CEO behaviours look like

*   where I think HR and HRDs have a gap

Before we move to the summary section, let's just recap on some of the aims and objectives that we set out in Chapter 1 to see how this chapter has informed us:

1. **To set out what HRDs can do to bring them back parity in the boardroom**

2. **Provide HRDs with the behaviours, competencies and skills required to really add value in the boardroom and to step-up**

3. **Understand why CEOs and Boards don't see HRDs in the CEO succession plan**

By going through this chapter, we have continued to answer some of the questions set above. It's clear that to enable HRDs to have parity, they must acquire and improve the behaviours that the top CEOs exhibit. In doing so, they should promote themselves to a higher level of visibility that hasn't existed before and give CEOs and Boards a different option that until now, just hasn't been there.

Summary and recap

The subject of this chapter was to look at the behaviours (skills, techniques, traits etc) of the top-performing and exceptional CEOs to allow us in HR to potentially change the way we behave.

To enable us to get to this we centred on three data points:

1. McKinsey's article on *What makes a CEO exceptional* (research on the top 600 CEOs from the S&P 500).

2. Harvard Business Review article looking at *What sets successful CEOs apart* (research on the Fortune 500 companies between 2000 and 2013).

3. Stephanie Chung's online article *10 Personality Traits Successful CEOs Share*.

There are probably many more articles on this subject, but for me, this was enough to get you to think about the end game. I was unable to find a published book or research that addressed this.

During the chapter, we looked at each element of the information that we had, and we asked the question:

"What's missing from HR and HRDs' kit bags?"

I have created a simple table that focusses on the behaviours that HR and HRDs need and, more importantly, what's missing:

Behaviour	What's missing
Objectivity	Using the data that we have in a way that matters at the top table to present clear and factual strategies to enable HR to be credible.
Objectivity	HR is often seen as too "fluffy" so HR needs to take the emotion out of the way that it puts forward new ideas and data without losing the human element from the equation.
Influence and Engaging for Impact	Direction change required – HR needs to evolve and address the lack of focus in what HR is all about, eg remember the research table in Chapter 1 that shows that only 28% of HR time is spent on true strategic partnering.
Influence and Engaging for Impact	HR people are by nature "people people", so while this is not missing, if we focused more on this advantage, imagine how influential HR could be.
Strategic Action/Thinking	Acting strategically with a total-company lens on.
Strategic Action/Thinking	Doing something different instead of implementing cost-reduction programmes that are a short-term fix but do nothing for the company's people, morale or external image.
Strategic Action/Thinking	HR's ability to look into the future, eg what will Artificial Intelligence and Robotics bring and what's the impact on employees, their families and companies?

Behaviour	What's missing
Organisational Balance	To set a high bar for the right performing people in HR teams that add true value. Time to look in the mirror! If we are going to make a difference, then we must have the right people with the right skills, qualifications and ongoing professional support and training.
Decision-Making and Conviction	All too often, HR looks for consensus at the top table and the lack of conviction means that change is slow and often based on old HR ways of doing things as it's the "safe" thing to do.
Adapting Proactively	The inability to do anything other than the norm – if it's not in the playbook, HR does nothing.
Adapting Proactively	Growth mindset!
Adapting Proactively	21st century approach rather than a 19th century one.
Delivering Reliably	Although HR does this, it's all too often seen as a drain on the organisation instead of being a profit centre and a success! Get out there and promote HR successes instead of waiting for someone else to do it.

Behaviour	What's missing
Project Management	Discipline and project management skills, i.e. regular meetings, data to inform decisions, planning. I would go a stage further and state that HR probably needs full-on project management training so that it speaks the same language as the rest of the business.
Understanding (Emotional Intelligence vs IQ)	Emotional Intelligence vs IQ: this should be "bread and butter" but I am not convinced that HR sees this as a behaviour it needs even though we train our employees in it.
Coaching vs Mentoring	The future of companies lies in coaching to enable the release of new ideas rather than the tried-and-tested. Again, HR is great at rolling this out but not so great at this for its own people.

Finally, it's clear that to enable HRDs to have parity, they must gain and or improve the behaviours that the top CEOs exhibit. In doing so, they will promote themselves to a higher level of visibility that hasn't existed before and give CEOs and Boards a different blueprint and options which previously did not exist or moreover, were overlooked.

In the next chapter we start to look at making the move from old to new.

CHAPTER 6

MAKING THE MOVE
FROM OLD TO NEW

If you recall back in Chapter 1 we touched on the story of Alicia in Marshall Goldsmith's book (**7**) *Triggers* (pp 94-95) and I promised that I would come back to this in this chapter due to its relevance to the topic.

Here's some context:

"For many companies, HR is solely an administrative responsibility – HR people are keepers of the employee handbook – with little influence over the company's direction and strategy. Not so at Alicia's company. With so many employees, the CEO knew that the decisions his Head of Human Resources made could make or break the organisation. The CEO told Alicia he was giving her a 'seat at the table.' Her job was as important as head of sales or chief operating officer."

What Alicia did next was really important, but I will come back to this a bit later in the chapter.

Wherever you turn now, it seems to be trendy, especially in 2018, to state that "HR is dead".

"What's wrong with HR?" as Lucy Adams asked in her book *HR Disrupted* (**4**). The best response that I've found is an online article by Human Resources Director Australia (HRDA) called "Is HR at Risk of Extinction?" (**29**) which stated:

"A global research study has predicted that the HR industry is at risk of extinction if it fails to rapidly reinvent itself."

The piece by HRDA basically stated that HR has lost its way and that the strategic direction of HR remains unclear. In addition, the article pulled out the following questions which HR is not addressing in today's world:

1. How do you maintain your culture?

2. How do you drive engagement across your organisation when your workforces are in different places, times and cultures?

And my all-time favourite quote for this chapter:

"HR is on the edge of a cliff and at real risk of falling over. They have two choices: either invent a way across the chasm or disappear into it."

The article then turns its attention to the increase in technology available to support HR and how the modern-day workforce is working increasingly with apps and other technology tools. It raises the question as to whether HR is applying this and engaging with the global mobile workforce.

"As time goes on, we will likely see some organisations get on with the process of reinvention and make the changes that are needed and reinvent their businesses to be able to adapt to the new world."

Wow! Is HR really on the edge? My answer is absolutely 100% yes! I agree with the above statements that HR is ripe for change, but it needs to change on a multitude of different levels, not just one. It would be very remiss of me not to at least bring some of Dave Ulrich's (**30**) work in here... and of course everyone knows who he is, right? In case you don't, here's what Wikipedia has to say about him:

*"**David Olson Ulrich** is a university professor, author, speaker, management coach, and management consultant. Ulrich is a professor*

of business at the Ross School of Business, University of Michigan and co-founder of The RBL Group.

"With his colleagues, he has written over 30 books that have shaped the HR profession, defined organisations as capabilities, and shown the impact of leadership on customers and investors. Ulrich served on the board of Directors for Herman Miller for seventeen years, and is a Fellow in the National Academy of Human Resources."

What's this got to do with charting the move from old to new? Well, let me draw you to a few words from a book that Dave Ulrich and colleagues wrote with Justin Allen, Wayne Brockbank, Jon Younger and Mark Nyman in 2009 called *HR Transformation – Building Human Resources from the Outside In* (**31**) (pp 55 to 56):

"The essence of a transformed HR department is the orientation to run the HR department like a business within a business. Any business has both a strategy (what it is trying to do) and a structure (how it organizes people and works to get things done).

"Both HR strategy and structure can be redesigned to make sure that the HR department responds to business context and delivers value to the organization."

Simply put, the authors then went on to say when looking at redesign – or what I would call evolution – you need to answer the following 3 questions:

1. Who are you? (vision)

2. What do you deliver? (mission or value proposition)

3. Why do you do it? (the results you want to achieve)

Later on in the book (p101) Ulrich and colleagues also call out the following, which interestingly backs up some of the comments which I made in Chapter 5:

"Ultimately, HR transformation depends on the quality of HR professionals."

They also stated:

"The competencies that were all that HR professionals once needed, are no longer sufficient in the new world of HR challenges."

Time to be controversial, so look out! Whilst I absolutely agree with what Ulrich *et al* wrote, I haven't seen it on a scale large enough to really make a difference. I wonder if Ulrich would agree with that statement? It's been nearly nine years since Ulrich's book came out, so what do you think? Is it just me?

Anyway, let's progress to what needs to happen for HR to make the move from old to new. It's my view that we must address the following magnificent challenges and levels. Six levels will be covered here in this chapter and the seventh will be covered in Chapter 7.

The Magnificent 7

1.   Schools to raise awareness of HR and its role through their career advisers and curriculum

2.   Colleges and universities should promote HR more

3.   Companies need to promote more HR apprenticeship opportunities

4.   Old HR institutes need be brought into the 21st century

5.   Old HR needs to become the New HR

6.   Old HRDs need to be the remodelled HRDs

7.   HRD need to cross the divide to CEO (see Chapter 7)

1. Schools to raise awareness of HR and its role through their career advisers and curriculum

OLD	NEW
Currently the role is non-existent, unless covered under the banner of Commerce or Business Studies.	The role of HR probably continues, perhaps covered in other associated subjects like Information Technology. Or it may become a subject in itself, aligned to "Business and Commerce of the Future". While humans exist, there will always be a need for companies to take "people decisions".
Within the present systems, choosing HR as a career is more likely to be suggested by the student than traditional careers advisers.	Careers advice – the role of HR needs to be given parity against other leadership roles in Accounts, IT etc. Also, we need to promote HR as a viable step to becoming a CEO of the future. Remove the barrier of 'Classic Careers' as they don't exist anymore in the 21st century.
Parent advocates (HR professionals) currently have limited involvement in schools' awareness delivery.	Parent advocates – as part of the CPD of HR professionals, it would be good to see parents incentivised, where possible, to engage with schools.
School boards currently are staying with the "same old, same old" approach to future curricula.	School boards need to keep an eye on what the future holds in terms of the roles required of our children and the next generation, balancing the curriculum to take into consideration the jobs of the future.

The change journey for HR, HRDs and the future CEO who comes from the ranks of HR, must start in the schools around the world. It is up to us to inspire our children and give them a different option; it's well put in the lyrics to the Witney Houston song, *The Greatest Love of All* (**32**):

"I believe that children are our future;

Teach them well and let them lead the way.

Show them all the beauty they possess inside.

Give them a sense of pride, to make it easier;

Let the children's laughter remind us how we used to be.

Everybody's searching for a hero;

People need someone to look up to."

Sorry, I couldn't resist putting that into the book and yes, I am a great fan of music of all genres.

2. Colleges and universities should promote HR more

OLD	NEW
Right now, HR is buried somewhere between Health and Humanities!	Either remove the "classic" career classifications and promote HR as a career of choice, or bring HR to the fore as one of the classic professions.
Even the best HR centric colleges and universities don't really promote the profession as one to aspire to.	HR needs to be on the front page of the prospectus, linked to real and tangible people.

OLD	NEW
Colleges and universities give limited exposure to companies where HR talent does exist not as part of the "milkround".	Colleges and universities need to allow HR professionals greater access as they do other professions such as Accountancy and IT.
No formal courses or training to become a CEO are currently offered.	New courses should be created having all the necessary professions at its core to empower more rounded CEOs of the future.
Presently, links to HR institutes are weak and methods of teaching HR are antiquated.	Connectivity between how HR is taught and connections to HR institutes around the world needs to improve massively.
The "victim mentality" is not addressed at college and university level, namely how HR is perceived in the workplace, which leads to a sense of not truly adding value.	Remove the stigma of how HR is perceived and enable a positive mindset that HR as a career is not the end point; it could be the starting point of a great career.
Lots of academic books on HR and HR strategy but without any clear cut direction set.	Colleges and universities need to work together with HR institutes to map out how HR is to work in the 21st century.

No song lyric this time, but I hope you can see what I am trying to get to here. HR must move on and colleges and universities must have a part in:

1. Getting young adults ready for an HR career.

2. Inspiring them that there is something else after HR.

3. Changing the antiquated 19th century way of doing HR into something that truly adds value, ie becoming a profit centre for businesses and not a drain on the bottom line.

3. Companies need to promote more HR apprenticeship opportunities

OLD	NEW
Very few companies have HR apprenticeship schemes, but they are out there, eg JCB and Toyota are two that I am personally aware of.	Companies around the world need to promote apprenticeships as a real option to young adults to progress while earning money and gaining valuable work experience.
Apprenticeships are not being promoted as an alternative to going to college or university.	Companies need to do more to encourage this approach. Going to college or university is not for everyone.
An old-fashioned mindset still exists in many companies around apprenticeships – perceived as non-value-add so it is paid lip service and a "token" HR person is brought in.	Companies need to let go of the tried-and-tested and embrace HR and what it can bring. It's a great opportunity to bring in the best and most talented future HRDs and CEOs if the apprenticeship cuts across all the functions as well as HR.

HR apprenticeships are a great way for companies to secure the best talent while the new HR apprentice works and is paid, gaining credible and real-life work experience. The apprentice is able to attend college or university as either a day-release scheme or evening classes. This way of studying should be something that is globally recognised in all areas, and not solely HR.

4. Old HR institutes need to be brought into the 21st century

OLD	NEW
Present HR institutes offer no clear direction or strategy on how HR is to evolve in the 21st century. Also, they need to answer the question as to whether HR is dead as a function or not.	North Star – the direction of travel has to come from somewhere and if it's not from someone in academia, then it has to come out of the HR institutions around the world as a joined-up strategic approach. For example, what is HR's role at the "top table"? Is it Strategic HR Business Partnering only, or does HR take away the admin burden from line management? What does HR start, stop, continue or add?
Qualifications are still based on the old ways of doing things.	Revision of HR qualifications needed to include the behaviours of the CEOs of the future. In addition, Project Management needs to be added into the qualifications, so if nothing else, basic PM training is given.
HR is still seen as the poorer cousins of other functions such as finance and IT.	In the immortal words of Paul McGee in his book *S.U.M.O. (Shut Up, Move On) - The Straight-Talking Guide to Succeeding in Life* (33) (pp 48-49), HR must stop wearing the "victim T-shirt" and instead start wearing the "S.U.M.O." one. Linked to Chapter 4 where we talked about the "growth mindset", I thought I would give you the following table which sets out the kind of language that HR needs to change.

Victim Language	Replace with S.U.M.O. Language
Life is not fair	I am unhappy about that, what can I do?
This is just the way I am	How can I improve?
There's nothing I can do	There's always something I can do
It's impossible	Let's find a way
Who is to blame?	How can we move forward?
I am a victim	I am a survivor
What's the point?	....

OLD	NEW
Continuous Professional Development (CPD) isn't where it should be; is it being given lip service I wonder?	CPD is a great way to drive HR and HRness forward, if lined up with research, further education, spending time out from your businesses, and spending time in other functions.
Old 19th century behaviours are the core basis of HR qualifications and studies (visit the CIPD website) to see the areas covered in the Profession Map (34) but in my opinion, even though it states the following, I am not convinced: *"The standards set out in the CIPD Profession Map, developed in collaboration with HR and L&D professionals, senior business people, academics and their organisations across the world, aim to set the bar high. They determine what the best HR and L&D professionals and organisations are doing, what they know and understand, to really make a difference and drive the performance of the organisation.* *"It has been designed to be relevant and applicable to HR professionals operating anywhere in the world, in all sectors and in organisations of all shapes and sizes."*	In the interests of keeping this section brief, it's clear from the Profession Map that things are missing when you refer back to Chapters 3, 4 and 5. Also, part of the Profession Map (and I touched on it above) must see HR people going outside of HR to gain valuable behaviours and skills which, allegedly, cannot be gained today. Without considering this, we won't be giving our HR colleagues the right skills for the future.
CIPD - more UK coverage than truly world-wide; what's the point of having a qualification or fellowship from the CIPD for instance?	I've been with the CIPD for several years and I am a great advocate of them and speak about them to my colleagues all around the world. However, more needs to be done to join up HR institutions under one umbrella to enable the profession to be truly recognised as a force to be reckoned with. Also, why isn't every HR person affiliated with an institute? The question "What's the benefit?" also needs to be answered.

OLD	NEW
Websites are, in my opinion, outdated and not as professional as those of other institutes.	This is just my view (and I am no website designer) but more and more can be achieved in this area. The global HR institutions need to see how other functions' institutes set out theirs and complete a gap analysis on what they need to do to get HR to the same place or better. Also, on the CIPD website, it claims to be: "setting the benchmark for excellence in HR and L&D for more than 100 years". I would be really interested to hear what you would say in this respect and does this sentence back up what I've written above?
No formal mentoring or buddy system exists for HR people with a desire to go further.	This is an area which can be quickly addressed, and I believe will do two things: 1) Give opportunities to those people in HR who have great career aspirations to connect with those HRDs who are at the top of the profession; and 2) Really give us a great view of what's happening with HR around the world and what areas of focus HR should be looking at.

Now I have been really critical of the CIPD here, only from a point of view that we need to move forward, and I am super passionate about what we do. Also just in case I have said something incorrectly, (and remember this is my opinion), I apologise in advance. Hopefully, I won't lose my fellowship because of this but if I do I will let you all know.

Incidentally, I did try to reach out to Peter Cheese, CEO of the CIPD via LinkedIn, but I never got a response and unfortunately, no acceptance of my request to connect either. It's a great shame as I would love to have got his perspective on some of the above.

5. Old HR needs to become the New HR

OLD	NEW
A victim mentality rules the day.	Covered in item 4 above – I can only stress that HR folks need to move on or be wiped out.
Unclear HR strategy on where HR is going and joined up though leadership.	HR together with colleges, universities and HR institutes need to set the guiding North Star for now. However, it cannot stay locked and needs to keep evolving as we go through this century to enable us to face the new challenges that the future will bring us. Everyone in HR needs to get behind it and make it happen.
HR professionals are, overall, non-aspirational when considering development areas outside of HR.	HR should look at cross-functional learning to safeguard the profession. In doing this, we will create HR leaders and teams that are truly commercial and add more value than HR does today.
Boards and existing CEOs don't see HR as a credible profession to deliver true value, return and business nous for their stakeholders. This is not surprising given the research in Chapter 1 which pointed at less than a third of HR's time being spent on strategy.	This incongruity needs to change. Remember the "war for talent" quote and what a company's greatest asset is: ie its people. Instead of "slash and burn" as a strategy for people, there should be focus on getting the right people at the right time and keeping them developed at the right level and pace applicable to that person. An engaged workforce truly adds commercial value and the stakeholders of businesses need to see this. HR does need to look at the Ulrich model and decide whether HR admin falls under HR, Global Business Solutions or another function which will support HR.
Boards and existing CEOs don't see HR leaders as business leaders.	Give boards and existing CEOs a different option; we've already seen in my research that the current CEO strategy is not working so why not open it up to HR?

OLD	NEW
HR is at a point of whether it dies or evolves.	While there is a human being in the workplace, HR cannot die but it does have to evolve. HR needs to catch-up quickly and over the next five years it has the opportunity to do this. The world is changing and it's time that HR changed too.
HRness has been downgraded and HR teams are managing on a shoestring budget while line managers are trying to become HR people overnight.	HR needs to focus on HRness and the people who work for us, investigating the future of new careers that are yet to be determined and enhancing employees' capabilities by treating them as human beings and not balance sheet numbers.

Recap on my definition of HRness:

"The people who work for us are really important and instead of paying lip service and downgrading HR, we should be enhancing our people capabilities. The focus shouldn't be solely on the financials or the new technology."

6. Old HRDs need to be the remodelled HRDs

OLD	NEW
It's too late to change.	It's never too late to change and to learn new skills, mindsets etc. Today's HR Directors have a responsibility to the profession, their teams and to the future HR professionals to make a positive change right now. There are new behaviours and things to learn such as commercialism. Spending time outside of HR in other functions will further enhance not only the companies of the future, but their employees and, more importantly, break the mould of future CEOs who can come from an HR background. Just imagine the difference that an HR person could bring to that role.

OLD	NEW
Not all HRDs are seen by their CEOs as being a trusted adviser.	To provide the balance for CEOs, HRDs must be on the opposite shoulder of the CFOs, and if that is not the case today, then ask yourself the question why not and do something about it. If you can't, perhaps it's time you moved to another role and started again.
HRDs are viewed by their organisations as solely the keepers of the employee handbook.	HRDs and HR are so much more than this so two things need to happen: 1) If your teams are viewed this way, what do you need to do to correct the perception? 2) What else should you be doing that you aren't yet?
HRDs' leadership training - good or bad?	HR is always really good at promoting learning in organisations, but it's time that we got better at receiving training ourselves. Whether it's soft- or hard-skills training shouldn't matter, but we need to see a sea-change in HRDs' leadership training.
HRDs are seen as "people people" with "emotional intellingence" but this isn't being utilised in the boardroom.	So much is written about emotional intelligence/quotient (EQ) and the absolute need for organisations in the future to look, not solely at IQ, but to view EQ as a way forward. This is especially true in regard to coaching being a pre-requisite of the future. Therefore, HRDs must promote EQ more in the boardroom. It's not a "soft and fluffy" tool at all, and if a CEO and his board don't have EQ, then they will be coming across as disconnected from their workforce.
HRDs aren't innovative	All too often, HRDs have stayed with the tried-and-tested but this needs to change in the future. It's time to rip up the old playbook and apply new lenses on what HR is trying to achieve in the future.

Summary and recap

During this chapter we have looked at the Magnificent 6 of the 7 areas where things need to move from old to new. Before we go through the summary, let's just check on the 7 aims of the book that we set out in Chapter 1:

1. Why is it almost impossible to move from an HRD role to a CEO, and what research, or more importantly, lack of research, has driven me to this write this book?

2. To set out what HRDs can do to bring back parity in the boardroom.

3. Why HRDs in general never make the transition to CEO while Board Members of other functions do?

4. Provide HRDs with the behaviours, competencies and skills required to really add value in the boardroom and to step-up.

5. Ultimately, consider what more broadly than HR needs to happen in order to make the jump to becoming a CEO ahead of their peers.

6. Understand why CEOs and Boards don't see HRDs in the CEO succession plan.

7. Why does the above still manifest itself as a consistent theme and why haven't Boards and CEOs realised the impact on those companies, their workforce and more importantly their bottom line as a result of this? Why have Boards and CEOs not embraced HRness?

This chapter touched on many of the aims listed above, eg Question 5: consider what more broadly than HR needs to happen in order to make the jump etc and Question 6: Understand why CEOs and Boards don't see HRDs in the CEO succession plans. These are two key questions that we have answered in this chapter.

The very first page of this section touched on the trendy narrative that "HR is dead" and picked up on the topical question, "Is HR at Risk of Extinction?" It appears that I am not alone in my thoughts around this, but one thing is clear: I may be the only one that is seeing the bigger picture and not focussing solely on one or two things that need fixing.

During the chapter we picked up on the work that Dave Ulrich *et al* did in their book *Building Human Resources from the Outside* (**34**) which specifically looked at three questions relating to HR redesign:

1. Who are you? (vision)

2. What do you deliver? (mission or value proposition)

3. Why do you do it? (the results you want to achieve)

We then looked at the Magnificent 7 areas and challenges where things need to move from old to new, but we only focused on the first 6, leaving the last for Chapter 7.

The Magnificent 7

1. Schools to raise awareness of the role of HR and careers advisers

2. Colleges and universities should promote HR more

3. Companies need to promote more HR apprenticeship opportunities

4. Old HR institutes need be brought into the 21st century

5. Old HR needs to become the New HR

6. Old HRDs need to be the remodelled HRDs

7. HRDs need to cross the divide to CEO (see Chapter 7)

The messages that I leave with you are:

- there is more than one action that needs to be taken

- there is more than one owner

- it will take a lot of commitment, energy and passion to move this forward globally

- does it need every level to work? Absolutely, however, as they say in the UK "you have to break a few eggs before you can make an omelette!"

In the next chapter, we look at how our HRDs move to become the CEOs of the future.

CHAPTER 7

MOVING FROM HRD TO CEO!

Over the course of the last 6 chapters, we have been really building to this point and of course, the reason for the book. Together we have looked at the skinny research on this topic, the articles, books, comments etc, so now let's try and look at what actually needs to happen to get you moving from HRD to CEO.

However, before we do, let's replay a few quotes from Martyn Phillips and Bill McDermott (Chapter 1):

Martyn:

> *"The skills and abilities of a good HR Director and those of a good CEO, they aren't that different. Both must be able to shape an organisation and achieve profitability through leveraging the workforce."*

Bill:

> *"Any CEO that doesn't put people first is leading a failed cause.*
>
> *"In the next five years, you'll see more chief human resources officers become CEOs than in the prior 50 years, because today you have to have people skills to succeed in business.*
>
> *"If you don't have people in your veins, in your DNA, you can't succeed."*

Hopefully that worked for you and it further inspired you to keep reading and learning.

Here we go then; let's look at how we move from being HRDs to CEOs by bringing together some of the things that we discussed during the course of this book.

Removing the barriers and blind spots

One of the biggest things that has come out through this book for me is that HRDs lack the desire to remove the barriers and blind spots to push past the chips on the shoulders and victim mentality. We can all sit here and moan about why life isn't treating us right; however, the ones who truly succeed are the ones that get off their backside and do something about it.

Included in this section, I would add that HR and HRDs need to have more drive in them to set their sights on something higher than just being an HRD (unless that's perfectly acceptable to you as a person of course, and good on you if this is the case.)

Let's sum up the barriers and blind spots that we talked about in this book and here's the list for you:

1. "Same old, same old" CEO profile

Boards and existing CEOs only see the blueprint of those CEOs who went before. They hide behind what the City might say if they bring in someone who hasn't delivered in a CEO or CFO role before; but what about those great HRDs out there that are truly adding value through company employees who are the backbone of any company? HRDs must step-up and demonstrate another option to Boards and existing CEOs. I appreciate that this might seem daunting, but if a Board cannot see the value that an HRD brings to a company, then that HRD is doing something very wrong and needs to move on.

I sincerely hope that there will be Board Members and CEOs reading this book too, so hopefully they will get the message loud and clear. If they don't, let me replay the following from Chapter 5 which was a *Harvard Business Review* entitled, "What sets successful CEOs apart" (**27**):

"From 2000 to 2013, about a quarter of the CEO departures in the Fortune 500 were involuntary, according to the conference board. The fallout from these dismissals can be staggering: forced turnover at the top costs shareholders an estimated $112 billion in lost value annually, a PwC study of the world's 2,500 largest companies showed. Those figures are discouraging for directors who have the hard task of appointing CEOs – and daunting to any leader aspiring to the C-suite."

2. Influence

HRDs need to really look at what their teams and HR strategy are doing for the companies of the future. HR cannot simply do the same as it's done before, and we need a 21st century HRness at the forefront. If HRDs do this and promote what they are doing and, more importantly, why they are doing it, I can see their "influence" stock in the boardroom go up by an exponential amount.

Throughout this book, we have looked at the research around where HR is spending the majority of its time and effort, and how controlling HR is when time and quality is at a premium to most companies. If you get a chance to read Lucy Adams' book *HR Disrupted* (**4**), I urge you to read pages 214 to 215 which back up the above comments. I don't totally agree with all of Lucy's comments relating to seats on the Board, but I do agree with her that things must change, and I completely agree with the final paragraph on page 215.

3. Business Experience

One consistent theme that kept coming up time and time again through my research was the assumption or perception that if you wanted to get to CEO, then you had to go outside of HR into areas of companies where there was a very real and credible responsibility for business delivery/budget/profitability and success. Why that isn't considered to be the case in HR is a different debate but it's probably because HR is not seen as a profit centre and is perceived as being a drain on the bottom line. Therefore, HRDs must:

1. Look to move outside of HR to gain the greater business acumen, or

2. Look to study and professionally qualify for the missing elements that HR doesn't cover today in greater details linked to what makes a CFO successful, or

3. Change the way that HR is run (new North Star); remember:

    • Who are you? (vision)

    • What do you deliver? (mission or value proposition)

    • Why do you do it? (the results you want to achieve so that it does become a profit centre). The company contracts – HR to add value where the business sees fit, instead of wasting time on items like performance management, which potentially add little value in return for the amount of time that is spent on the processes and procedures that sit around it.

- Professionally formalise Continual Professional Development in HR rather than paying it lip service.

4. Bring the Human/HRness back into HR and Companies

CEOs of the future must be emotionally connected to their companies' people, aware of the impact on their bottom line and that having a demotivated and uninspired workforce will damage a company, not only financially but reputationally too; ultimately they are responsible for treating employees fairly and appropriately especially in how CEOs and business leaders lead, manage and have an impact on their people.

Remember back in Chapter 1 where we talked about the CEO of Uber having to resign because of alleged staff abuse? Also, recall what Rolls Royce did when they wanted to reinvigorate themselves; they put in an HRD who had no direct experience of HR!

HRDs have this human focus already in their DNA, but there is more that current HRDs can do to raise the bar higher and higher. Boards and CEOs need to recognise this and allow their current HRDs to teach them on how to do it better. A great example of this for those people reading this book and love NFL football, check out the online article by Doug Pederson (coach of 2018 Super Bowl winners, Philadelphia Eagles) (**35**) where he touches on the following 6 principles:

1.   *Practice self-awareness in order to achieve Emotional Intelligence.*

2.   *Exercise empathy – put yourself in your team members' shoes, look through their lens.*

3.   *Create a culture of transparency – stay visible and grow trusted by your team.*

4.   *Invest time in the relationships you have with your team members and give freedom for relationships to grow between them.*

5.   *Never allow adversity to get you and your team down – change the narrative to see challenges as opportunities.*

6.   *Provide a purpose higher than self. Give your team the opportunity to align with something mission-driven, it will elevate them.*

I am a fan of taking great leadership examples from sport into business and I think that Doug lists some really fantastic EI (EQ) items above; well done to the Philadelphia Eagles for an amazing win and self-belief.

5.   Leadership development for HRDs

Have you ever heard the saying, "Do as I say, not as I do?"

HR is really great at generating development for other people and functions, however, in my experience HR and

HRDs are not, for whatever reason, taking this seriously and applying the same leadership development study and training to HR.

I know that I am generalising here, and I know that I am tarring everyone with the same brush, but I'd be interested in knowing how far off the mark I really am. Email me if you disagree. If I am right, then this is a simple barrier or blind spot that can be removed pretty quickly. In doing so, we do need the likes of the CIPD to really look at how HR and HRDs are being trained today, and as we touched on in Chapter 6, really focus on the missing behaviours and 21st century training that HR and HRD needs in the future.

6. HR and HRD being a career choice

If you cast your memory back to Chapter 2, we looked at the different ways that people ended up in HR and then made the move to being HRD or Head of HR. The biggest barrier or blind spots for me centred on schools, colleges and universities where HR, HRD and the jump to CEO is not a career path that is made visible to our young people.

We had some great examples where people "fell" into HR or went to university for something different and then ended up in HR via a graduate scheme. Now please don't think that I am putting any of these routes down at all; it merely tells you the story that on the whole, HR doesn't get the air time that some of the classic careers get. Why is this a barrier or blind spot to stop HRDs from moving to CEO? I hear you asking.

Simply put, I believe that you need to *plan* your way through a career to the top, and the best people I know who do make it to the top are passionate about their careers and the knowledge that they have gained along the way. Therefore, HRDs need to address this with the help of HR institutions like the CIPD.

This one is going to take time, but that doesn't mean we shouldn't start this change now. Come on academia and the CIPD! This is one that we must crack together. If nothing else, can we urge the CIPD to look critically at their website and compare to those of other institutions like the ACA, ACCA and CIMA?

7. Parity with other functional Heads in the boardroom

In Chapter 3 we looked at how other functions grow their leaders. Memory jog – the Robert Half research stated that almost one in four CEOs were chartered accountants. The others were made up of retail, engineering, marketing and technology backgrounds. It's clear that HRDs need to do more in the boardroom to gain parity and this isn't something that will change overnight either. However, it is clear that this is one blind spot or barrier that absolutely needs to change. HRDs have the people data, skills, experience and knowledge to do this, so ask yourself: what's stopping us? After all, if you look at the pressures of the other functions, HR is no different. Cast your mind back to Darren Lees' comments in Chapter 3:

"In my view only when companies and organisations see their people as their key assets and their unique selling points, (and that is

recognised by the City as much as financial delivery and shareholder value creation which again is often financially linked) will we see more HR executives taking the CEO role, versus today."

8. Embrace the growth mindset

Earlier in this chapter, we commented that HR needs to move forward and remove the blocks and barriers, especially when we look at "I stick to what I know!" During Chapter 4, we investigated the Fixed vs Growth Mindset that exists with CEOs, Boards, HR and HRDs.

It wasn't a surprise to me that most of the answers to the questions came back with the same conclusion – that all parties landed firmly in the "fixed" box!

I'm not going to regurgitate the whole chapter but if you are HRD, a Board Member or an existing CEO, I leave it to you to really look in the mirror and move to the growth mindset rather than staying with the fixed. This is one easy blind spot and barrier to remove, but it will need you to really critically examine your own reality; if you find that you scored yourself in the growth mindset box, just do me a favour and check with the people who really will not lie to you and are brave when giving developmental feedback, as it's very easy to think something different.

9. Modelling the behaviours of the great CEOs

During Chapter 5, we looked at the exceptional traits of high-performing CEOs with the view of removing the barriers and blind spots to enable our HRDs to move to CEO. If you recall, we looked at what was missing from HR and HRDs' kit bags. We already touched on "Influencing" above, so I'm not going to go over that again. However, it does re-enforce how much influence plays, not only at CEO level, but I believe generally at all levels, whether in business or in your personal life. The other areas that came out were:

1. **Objectivity** – HR has a wealth of data which we seemingly don't do anything with, so HRDs need to do more in this space with their CEOs and Boards.

2. **Acting strategically** – HRDs need to advise and guide companies with a total-company lens on and the ability to do something different instead of, for example, the traditional, "Let's cut costs and worry about our people later" (21st century solutions).

3. **Organisational balance** – HRDs need to look at their function and challenge themselves by asking, "Is your HR function set up with the right performing people and, if not, what are you doing about it?" At CEO level, this is a critical skill when stepping into a new role and having the right team to support you is crucial to the success of any company. HRDs need to be able to demonstrate that they are able to lead high-performing teams.

4. **Deciding with speed and conviction** – The biggest barrier that HRDs have is that they try to seek consensus and as a result this can come across as lacking conviction. This is invariably

tied to HR doing more of the old stuff and, as such, HRDs need to be more forthright in knowing what's best when it comes to people matters.

5. **Engaging for impact** – This behaviour should be a no-brainer for HRDs. This shouldn't be a barrier nor a blind spot as all good HRDs should see the value of being able to engage with people in the business, its stakeholders and in the role of the CEO, its shareholders.

6. **Adapting proactively** – I am going to link this back to our earlier point 8 and growth mindset. Clearly, this is a must when it comes to being a Growth Minded CEO and there's no reason why HRDs shouldn't possess this mindset.

7. **Delivering reliably** – When has HR ever not delivered reliably? I hear you ask. My answer is that it probably hasn't – it's just that the people at the top table never recognised it, and as a result, it's never been appreciated. HRDs need to find a way of promoting what HR does, but before they do that, they need to evaluate the HR North Star and what HRness means to the company that they work for.

8. **Reading people and adapting to necessary management styles** – HRDs need to come back to the North Star for HR and recognise that people are all very different. CEOs have the ability to read people and adapt but I am not sure that HRDs can – or if they can, perhaps they are

just afraid to break the mould of the tried-and-tested.

9. **Coaching vs Mentoring** – This for me isn't just for HRDs who have aspirations of becoming CEOs: it's for everyone. The world is changing and to enable the release of new ideas and innovation, we can't simply roll out the same old, same old.

10. Magnificent 6 of 7 Old to New things that must change

We covered this in chapter 6; however, I cannot stress enough that I truly believe that HR can change the world if all of the items that I listed are addressed. Ideally I would like to see all of these tackled but I know that some will move faster than others. There's also an accountability piece here that the relevant parties need to embrace. It MUST start with HR now as this is totally within our gift to do. Please refer back to chapter 6 if you need to refresh your memory of what these are.

It's time to put that growth mindset to work and "seize the day".

Summary and recap

This chapter brought together what the previous 6 chapters uncovered regarding the barriers and blind spots that prevent HRDs from becoming CEOs of the future. We started the chapter with two sets of quotes from Martyn Phillips and Bill McDermott which spelt out in their own words why HRDs would make great CEOs.

Following this, we went on to list out the 10 main areas that would need to be removed or improved by the multi-players. These players range from schools all the way through to Boards and CEOs and they are pivotal to enabling HRDs to make the move.

The main barriers and blind spots are:

1. Same old, same old CEO profile – let's change the CEO blueprint!

2. Influence – HR can't simply do what its done for the last 100 years – we can influence the Board's direction so let's make this happen.

3. Business Experience – to enable the move to become a CEO, HRDs do need to be credible in the commercial space so either a move into a business role or another functional role should be considered. This should be addressed in the North Star strategy.

4. Bring the Human/HRness back into HR and companies – people argue that we are still in the recession, so this is absolutely required. CEO's and Boards cannot continue to ignore that HRness is required.

5. Leadership development for HR and HRDs – it's time that HR took a good look at this; to improve this must change as again, how can HR be credible if it doesn't address this point? This is an easy fix.

6. HR and HRD being a career choice – why not?
    Working in HR is something that I truly enjoyed,
    and I've had the great opportunity of travelling
    the world and working with great people and
    great cultures. It's made me a better person and
    exposed me to things I would never have learned
    just working in the UK. We can change but we
    do need the HR Institutions and schools etc to do
    this too.

7. Parity with other functional heads in the
    boardroom – HR has as much right in the
    boardroom as any other function or business
    component; HR must believe this and make the
    change.

8. Embrace the Growth Mindset – this should not
    be a fad or the latest craze! Instead it should
    be the mantra for HR and included in the new
    North Star strategy. In the meantime, you the
    reader can change or re-enforce your mindset
    today.

9. Modelling the behaviours of the great CEOs
    – remember the 9 main areas which are the
    minimum! Tackle these and you will be well on
    your way.

10. Magnificent 6 of 7 Old to New things that must
    change! It's up to you to make the difference and
    be the catalyst.

Yes, it is a long shopping list of things that would need to happen however, to be honest with you, there's nothing there that can't be achieved. The real question is: who wants to grab it, run with it and above all reach that level that was, for the majority, unattainable before?

Before signing off this chapter, let me give you this quote from Sir Edmund Hillary which I believe sums this up:

"It's not the mountain that we conquer but ourselves."

Now to Chapter 8 which I called "The world is your oyster!"

CHAPTER 8

THE WORLD IS
YOUR OYSTER

I absolutely believe this to be the case and with the right mindset anything is possible. We have covered a huge amount of content over the last 7 chapters. While I don't expect this chapter to take up masses of time and words, I did want to make sure that we looked at the 7 aims that we set out back in Chapter 1 to ensure that we covered everything that we had to. I've purposely left space before my intentionally short answer so that you can write your own answers

1. **Why is it almost impossible to move from an HRD position to a CEO and what research, or more importantly, lack of research, has driven me to this book?**

Today from the research that I have been able to uncover, (I would have thought there would have been more), it's very difficult for HRDs in their current form to make the move from HRD to CEO. We have covered the many reasons why and they range from HRDs not fitting the current mould to the City's view of tried-and-tested (the traditional blueprint), through to HR just not having the behaviours that are seemed to be required at the top level.

2. How to set out what HRDs can do to bring them back parity in the boardroom.

As we have seen in the previous chapter, there are ten main areas that have to be tackled in order give HRDs parity in the boardroom. Not all of these can be achieved by HRDs and HR alone. There are other players like schools, colleges, universities, HR Institutions, shareholders, Boards, CEOs and of course you, who also have a part to play in this. However, if the changes were implemented, imagine what the new world might look like with an HRD or at least someone who has been exposed to purist HR in the top job. We dare to dream!

3. Why do HRDs in general never make the transition to CEO whilst other functions' Board Members do?

There's a very clear stigma against HR and it stems from schools and the so-called classic careers (of which HR isn't one today.) There is a view in the other functions that HR and HRDs in particular don't have the relevant clout, behaviours or company gravitas to warrant the top job, which, of course, is completely incorrect. As we have seen in the previous chapters, HRDs don't fit the current CEO blueprint, so no surprises why HRDs don't make the transition to CEO. However, as we have also seen through the research, billions of dollars are being wasted by the traditional approach, so it's time for a change.

4. Provide HRDs with the behaviours, competencies and skills required to really add value in the boardroom and to step-up.

My hope is that we have together looked at the behaviours, competencies and skills required by HRDs by looking at the research around the top-performing CEOs (remember modelling yourself on a successful person is a great idea no matter what you are trying to achieve).

We also looked at the relevant actions that need to happen which will support an HRD's route to becoming a CEO. However, we haven't just looked at this with an HRD lens on. We've taken a view on each level that needs to be tackled starting with the schools and colleges all the way up to Boards and CEOs.

5. **Ultimately consider what more broadly than HR needs to happen in order to make the jump to becoming a CEO ahead of one's peers.**

I think we smashed this one and we've made a great start on what needs to happen or to change to enable the jump to becoming a CEO for HRDs. The only challenge is that it's not something that is fully in the gift of HR and HRDs; however, with the right effort and commitment it is possible.

6. Understand why CEOs and Boards don't see HRDs in the CEO succession plan.

It's an absolute blind spot and to a certain degree lethargy. To be honest, this isn't just an issue for CEOs and Boards either. HR, schools, HR institutions and other functional institutions all have a hand in how HR is perceived and where it sits within the so-called classic careers.

Simply put, I don't think anyone's ever truly challenged this, but now is the right time. I sincerely hope that we have Board Members reading this book.

7. **Why does the above still manifest itself as a consistent theme and why haven't Boards and CEOs realised the impact on their companies, their workforce and, more importantly, their bottom line as a result of this? Why have Boards and CEOs not embraced HRness?**

It's a great question, don't you agree, as to why this has never been addressed before on a larger scale? It has happened, but in a piecemeal way which, for whatever reason, sadly never got the traction to carry it forward. I am hoping that Boards and CEOs see this as a massive opportunity to do something amazing; only time will tell but to quote my wife's old school motto:

"From little acorns, mighty oak trees grow."

There you go folks that's the end of Chapter 8 and I really hope that this brought it all back to you. I'm not going to summarise or recap the chapter as I think you get it all now. Right? It's your time to take this to the next level so step-up and make a difference right now.

You are almost at the end of the book so the last main chapter is all about my closing observations. Please read on.

CHAPTER 9

CLOSING
OBSERVATIONS

When I first envisaged writing this book, my ultimate aim was to be a catalyst for change, to provide an insight into what skills and behaviours need to be developed and promoted to enable people in the world of Human Resources to aspire to and become CEOs. However, in the process of writing it all down, I now realise that this may not be for everyone in HR and it is going to be down to the individual to decide whether to aim high or not.

Ultimately HR needs to change in the future if it's ever going to survive – and I do mean *survive*. That said, wouldn't it be great to see a CEO who had an HR background, or at least a qualification in HR, in a FTSE 100 company or in other global indexes within the next few years? Who knows it might just be YOU! I sure hope so.

In addition, I realise that my mindset has changed slightly, insomuch that I hope this book will inform Boards and CEOs who don't have an HR background to seek out HRness! However, unless this change happens, companies and organisations will never truly realise their full potential across the globe. Moreover, instead we will only have a few that will ever make the evolutionary jump to becoming the best companies and organisations to work for that are still financially sound and fit for the future.

I ask HR institutions around the world to look at what the profession should be doing in the 21st century. Critically, they need to take the lead and set the North Star that is missing today.

It is ironic but encouraging that at the time of writing this, I received an email (including a survey) from Victoria

Winkler, the Director of Professional Development of CIPD that stated:

"We want to hear from you about the knowledge and behaviours that you draw on to make an impact in your role, as part of a member-wide consultation on our new professional standards.

"That's why we're creating new standards for the people profession – focused on the future, setting out who we are and what we stand for, as well as the unique knowledge and behaviours that make us the experts on people, work and change."

It's a start in the right direction but as my old schoolteacher Mr Green used to say, "Could try harder," and I am sincerely hoping that HR institutions like the CIPD will step-up and take notice.

To my colleagues in other functions like finance and IT, I would challenge you to look at this book and drive your professions to include more HRness. Who knows, in years to come there may not be separate functions any more; instead, there will exist a standard function called something like "Company Support" where we have people who are cross-functional leaving schools, apprenticeships, colleges and universities with a combined finance, HR, IT and sales education, and these will be the CEOs of the future.

Finally, HR can change the world and I firmly believe that HR and HRDs can be the leaders of the future.

Please do write to me to let me know what you think of the book; it's all part of the growth mindset to improve and learn.

Can you imagine an HRD being *your* next CEO? *I can and so should you!*

Now go and make the difference – good luck.

Bibliography

1. http://www.hrmagazine.co.uk/article-details/is-a-move-from-hr-director-to-chief-executive-a-bridge-too-far

2. https://www.theglobeandmail.com/report-on-business/careers/leadership-lab/why-hr-expertise-is-a-critical-addition-to-your-board/article34986443/

3. https://en.wikipedia.org/wiki/War_for_talent

4. Adams, Lucy, *HR Disrupted* (Practical Inspiration Publishing, 2017)

5. https://www.google.co.uk/search?q=meaning+of+homongenous&sourceid=ie7&rls=com.microsoft:en-GB:IE-Address&ie=&oe=&gfe_rd=cr&dcr=0&ei=vdNWWsaSCe6fwALqwJnwDA

6. https://en.oxforddictionaries.com/definition/blind_spot

7. Goldsmith, Marshall *Triggers: Sparking positive change and making it last* (Profile Books, 2016)

8. Lawler III, Edward E and Boudreau, John W, *Achieving Excellence in Human Resources Management – An Assessment of Human Resources Functions* (Stanford Books, 2015)

9. People Management Magazine, *How to Be Top Dog – What great HR leaders do and how to follow in their footsteps!* (CIPD, March 2017)

10. Lawler III, Edward E and Boudreau, John W, *Achieving Excellence in Human Resources Management – An Assessment of Human Resources Functions* (Stanford Books, 2009)

11. http://www.hrmagazine.co.uk/article-details/is-a-move-from-hr-director-to-chief-executive-a-bridge-too-far

12. https://www.businesslive.co.za/bt/opinion/2017-06-24-arthur-goldstuck-uber-chaos-brings-humanity-to-depersonalised-tech

13. https://en.wikipedia.org/wiki/Association_of_Chartered_Certified_Accountants

14. https://www.theguardian.com/careers/forums-best-of-the-forums

15. http://www.telegraph.co.uk/business/2018/01/02/rolls-royce-kickstart-turnaround-executive-shake-up/

16. https://en.wikipedia.org/wiki/Harald_Kr%C3%BCger

17. https://en.wikipedia.org/wiki/Tim_Cook

18. https://www.icas.com/ca-today-news/one-in-four-ceos-are-chartered-accountants

19. https://www.roberthalf.co.uk/press/ftse-100-companies-want-homegrown-technology-talent-top-role-reveals-robert-half

20. http://www.dnb.com/perspectives/finance-credit-risk/4-trends-in-role-of-modern-finance-leader.html

21. https://www.icaew.com/en/technical/personal-development/leadership/great-finance-leaders-should-win-hearts-and-minds

22. Syed, Matthew, *Black Box Thinking: Marginal Gains and the Secrets of High Performance* (John Murray, 2016)

23. https://en.oxforddictionaries.com/definition/behaviour

24. https://www.mckinsey.com/business-functions/strategy-and-corporate-finance/our-insights/what-makes-a-ceo-exceptional

25. https://en.wikipedia.org/wiki/S%26P_500_Index

26. https://www.cipd.co.uk/podcasts/look-ahead-2018

27. https://hbr.org/2017/05/what-sets-successful-ceos-apart

28. https://www.inc.com/stephanie-chung/10-personality-traits-every-ceo-should-have.html

29. https://www.hcamag.com/hr-news/is-hr-at-risk-of-extinction-246035.aspx

30. https://en.wikipedia.org/wiki/Dave_Ulrich

31. Ulrich, Dave, Allen, Justin, Brockbank, Wayne, Younger, Jon, Nyman, Mark, *HR Transformation: Building Human Resources From the Outside In* (McGraw Hill Books, 2009)

32. http://www.songfacts.com/detail.php?lyrics=3977

33. McGee, Paul, *S.U.M.O. (Shut Up, Move On)* (TJ International Ltd, 2016)

34. https://www.cipd.co.uk/cipd-hr-profession/cipd-hr-profession-map/default.html

35. https://www.linkedin.com/pulse/lead-emotional-intelligence-6-ways-doug-pederson-head-dudley/?trk=eml-email_feed_ecosystem_digest_01-recommended_articles-17-Unknown&midToken=A QEhN787jEksAA&fromEmail=fromEmail&ut=28b L9sChH5e881

36. https://hbr.org/2014/12/why-chief-human-resources-officers-make-great-ceos

37. https://www.morganmckinley.co.uk/article/will-your-next-ceo-come-hr

38. https://www.quora.com/How-difficult-is-it-to-be-a-CEO

39. https://www.theglobeandmail.com/report-on-business/careers/leadership-lab/why-hr-expertise-is-a-critical-addition-to-your-board/article34986443/

About the author

At the tender age of 50, I am still evolving as a person and happily embracing the "growth mindset" and continual learning. I guess, like everyone, there's a back story and mine starts in a little village called Llanbradach in South Wales in the UK. Born with a cleft palate, I shouldn't have really survived but I did; as a child I was never in great health due to one thing or another.

School was not great for me personally, although I left with one good O-Level in commerce which set me on the path towards HR. At sixteen, I joined a Youth Training Scheme in Office Management. It wasn't what I wanted to do at all when I was in school; instead I had wanted to go to the Royal Air Force's Music Academy and take a second role in the Military Police.

However, nearly 33 years on, I really love working in HR and I've made a very great career out of doing something that I really and genuinely like doing. Hopefully, this is evident by the fact that I have an MSc in Payroll and Business Management, the dual Fellowships of the CIPD and the Chartered Institute of Payroll Professional.

I married my wife Debs in 2000 (and still madly in love with her) and all together, we have three children, Cadence 11, Megan 25 and Evan 26, and to date we have two grandchildren, Logan and Deacon.

For the last six years, I have been working as a freelance HR consultant for some great companies including Bank of America, HSBC, Ecolab and Imperial Brands in multi-discipline strategic and operational roles across the world. Prior to this I was employed by Eversheds LLP, Accenture, Koorb (NZ) and E.ON as well as numerous other companies which you can see on my LinkedIn page and on my website: GGJ Global Consulting Ltd., www.ggjglobalconsulting.com.

Careerwise, I am still working my way to becoming a future CEO and evolving my own HR consultancy business to ensure that I continually add value to my clients, now and in the future. However, I am passionate about coaching, Emotional Intelligence and company evolution, which I hope is apparent in the contents of this book.

In my personal life, I totally enjoy spending time with my family; I meditate when I can to ensure that I keep myself grounded, and I really enjoy getting out and about with our two dogs, walking and hiking in the Peak District.

Where do I go from here? Well, having written this book, I hope that I will be able to convert this into a PhD by taking the research on to the next level. If I do, watch this space – you never know, I might be interviewing you next.

Have fun, and I sincerely hope that you enjoyed reading this book, and, if nothing else, I hope it's opened up your mind to other options and/or new career path.

For the business world, my desire is that this book changes the traditional approach to who becomes a CEO.

Can you imagine an HRD being *your* next CEO? *I can and so should you!*

Printed in Great Britain
by Amazon